"A very accessible and informed guide to this magisterial English translation of the Bible. Few will fail to benefit from its wisdom and learning."
Alister McGrath, Chair in Theology, Ministry, and Education; Head of the Centre for Theology, Religion, and Culture, Kings College, London

"What a treat—the leading evangelical scholar on the Bible as literature discussing the Bible translation that is probably the greatest achievement in English literature! Ryken tells the story of how the King James Version came into being and describes its wide-ranging impact over the last four hundred years, while frankly contrasting the literary merits of the KJV with some of the modern translations. This is an important topic treated well. I found it riveting and edifying."
Ray Van Neste, Associate Professor of Biblical Studies; Director, R. C. Ryan Center for Biblical Studies, Union University

"Who would be more qualified to write the definitive study of the history, stylistic excellence, and pervasive influence of the King James Bible than a distinguished professor of English, Milton scholar, expert on Puritanism, and authority on the Bible as literature? Professor Ryken fills the bill, and he has produced an exemplary work: its research is extensive, its scholarship is impressive, its argument is reasonable, and its readability makes it accessible to scholar and layperson alike."
D. G. Kehl, Professor of English Emeritus, Arizona State University; author, *The Literary Style of the Old Bible and the New*

"The story of the making of the King James Bible has been told before, but given popular misconceptions it deserves retelling. An especially valuable feature of Leland Ryken's *The Legacy of the King James Bible* for many readers will be Ryken's rich description of the translation's literary and cultural impact, as well as his examination of key questions too many take for granted: what makes a Bible literary, and what constitutes this Bible's remarkable prose and poetic style?"
Hannibal Hamlin, Associate Professor of English, The Ohio State University; coeditor, *The King James Bible after Four Hundred Years*

"Leland Ryken skillfully traces the King James Version's powerful influence on the history, culture, and literature of the English-speaking peoples. Drawing upon a lifetime of scholarship in both English literature and the Bible, Ryken has written a valuable volume celebrating the most important book in the English language."

Diane Lynn Severance, Director, Dunham Bible Museum,
Houston Baptist University

"Leland Ryken is eminently qualified to write a book on the legacy of the King James Bible. His years of teaching sixteenth- and seventeenth-century English literature and his extensive writings on the Bible as literature and familiarity with modern English translations put him in the seat of profound authority. His personal acquaintance with the text of the KJV from a very early age gives his delightful stories a ring of authenticity. Dr. Ryken will lead you into a deep appreciation of this four-hundred-year-old translation—the beauty of its language, its undeniable influence on American and English culture, and its molding of literary personalities, poets, musicians, and yes, even politicians. Once I began reading Ryken's book, I couldn't put it down. It will tempt you to go to your bookshelf, blow the dust off your KJV, and begin reading it again. Ryken has clearly and precisely demonstrated what has made it such an enduring cultural phenomenon—the simplicity of its prose, the beauty of its poetry, the cadence of its diction, and the grandeur of its message."

Donald L. Brake, Dean Emeritus, Multnomah Biblical
Seminary; author, *A Visual History of the King James Bible*

"Leland Ryken comes not to bury the King James Bible at its four hundredth birthday, although he knows full well it may be dying. He comes not to praise the King James Bible, although he is fully alive to its astonishing beauty, teachings, and influence. He comes simply to document a fundamental truth we must never forget: that the KJV was the best translation of many great translations in its own day and that even if it dies tomorrow in a world that seems to have lost both its inner and outer ears, it will live on forever through its words reflected in the work of some of the greatest musicians, painters, poets, preachers, playwrights, and prose writers of all time."

Al Elmore, Professor of English and Drama,
Athens State University

THE LEGACY OF THE
KING JAMES BIBLE

OTHER CROSSWAY BOOKS BY LELAND RYKEN

The Word of God in English:
Criteria for Excellence in Bible Translation

Bible Translation Differences:
Criteria for Excellence in Reading and Choosing a Bible
Translation

Choosing a Bible:
Understanding Bible Translation Differences

Translating Truth:
The Case for Essentially Literal Bible Translation
(with Wayne Grudem, C. John Collins, Vern S. Poythress,
and Bruce Winter)

ESV Literary Study Bible
(coedited with Philip Graham Ryken)

Preach the Word:
Essays on Expository Preaching: In Honor of R. Kent Hughes
(coedited with Todd Wilson)

Understanding English Bible Translation:
The Case for an Essentially Literal Approach

THE LEGACY OF THE KING JAMES BIBLE

CELEBRATING 400 YEARS OF THE MOST INFLUENTIAL ENGLISH TRANSLATION

LELAND RYKEN

CROSSWAY

WHEATON, ILLINOIS

The Legacy of the King James Bible: Celebrating 400 Years of the Most Influential English Translation

Cover design: Studio Gearbox
Cover photo: iStock & Photos.com

First printing 2011
Printed in the United States of America

Trade paperback ISBN:	978-1-4335-1388-6
PDF ISBN:	978-1-4335-1389-3
Mobipocket ISBN:	978-1-4335-1390-9
ePub ISBN:	978-1-4335-2451-6

Library of Congress Cataloging-in-Publication Data
Ryken, Leland.
    The legacy of the King James Bible : celebrating 400 years of the most influential English translation / Leland Ryken.
        p. cm.
    Includes bibliographical references and index.
    ISBN 978-1-4335-1388-6 (tp)
    1. Bible. English—Versions—Authorized—History. 2. Bible—Influence. I. Title.
    BS186.R95 2011
    220.5'2038—dc22

                                                                                    2010033000

Crossway is a publishing ministry of Good News Publishers.

VP		22	21	20	19	18	17	16	15	14	13	12	11
14	13	12	11	10	9	8	7	6	5	4	3	2	1

For Jim Wilhoit,
colleague par excellence

CONTENTS

Contents

PREFACE

THE PUBLICATION OF THE KING JAMES BIBLE in 1611 was a landmark event in the English-speaking world. In fact, I tell students in my English literature courses that it was *the* major event in English and American literature. Perhaps the importance is even greater than that: what has influenced the whole history of England and America more than the King James Bible?

The year 2011 marks the four hundredth anniversary of the publication of the King James Version of the Bible. It is customary to mark the anniversaries of public events with ceremonies and books. When a college or church reaches a milestone like a hundredth anniversary of its founding, we can confidently expect a book to accompany the event. In the realm of literature and the arts, every year sees the honoring of authors, composers, artists, or masterworks with performances, exhibits, and books.

The fanfare accompanying anniversaries like the ones I have mentioned is partly honorific, designed to praise what is praiseworthy and give honor where honor is due. But the impulse to commemorate anniversaries goes beyond that. When important people, places, or events are elevated in our consciousness, we naturally become curious to know the facts about them. When

I visit a literary or historical site in England or America, I not infrequently leave with a book or pamphlet in my hand. Numerous events, exhibits, and books are expected to celebrate the four hundredth anniversary of the King James Bible. It could hardly be otherwise. Inquiring minds want to know, and there is no good reason for cynicism about the attention that the King James Bible will receive around the time of its anniversary.

The book that you are holding in your hands has been occasioned by the four hundredth anniversary of the King James Bible. My primary purpose in writing the book is to provide information about the King James Bible and its influence. Alister McGrath, in the preface to his book *In the Beginning: The Story of the King James Bible and How It Changed a Nation, a Language, and a Culture*, states that he wrote the book simply to answer the questions that arose over half a century of living with a King James Bible that he had received as a child (as did every other child in England in 1953 by command of Queen Elizabeth II upon her coronation). The impulse behind my book is similar: I want as many people as possible to know the story of the King James Bible and its influence.

I have not regarded it as a leading purpose to praise the King James Bible. Its nature and legacy speak for themselves. What is in danger of being lost (or has already been lost) is the story of what the King James Bible is and how it has influenced the English-speaking world. We do not need adulation of the KJV; we need knowledge of the things that have produced the adulation through the centuries.

While it is not my *purpose* to praise the King James Bible, I have made no effort to withhold my positive assessment of it. Its excellencies are part of the information that I want to make plain. I hope that my book will serve the same purpose as books that I have purchased after visiting Shakespeare's Stratford or Lucy Maud Montgomery's Prince Edward Island—to explain what makes them so famous and to share a legitimate enthusiasm about them.

We live in an era of revisionism and debunking. This has predictably infiltrated attitudes toward the KJV. If for no other reason than that it is the most influential and revered English Bible that has ever existed, the King James Bible is on the "hit list" of cultural revisionists. As I read the statements of debunkers of the KJV, I am at a loss to ascertain what it is that these writers have against the King James Bible, with the possible exception that the King James Bible is "sonorous." I am reminded of a statement that C. S. Lewis made about the sixteenth-century humanists: they jeer but do not refute.

A favorite ploy of revisionists and debunkers is to label any positive statement about an author or book "hagiographic," with the implication that hagiography is a criminal act. I was shocked to see a reviewer of McGrath's book on the KJV dismiss it as hagiographic. An obvious feature of his book is its informational and objective approach to the material.

A brief history of my own contact with the KJV is as follows. I still have in my possession a King James Bible bearing this inscription in the front: "Presented to Leland Ryken by Father and Mother on December 25, 1951." I was nine years old. The gold-embossed title "Holy Bible" is nearly illegible on the leather-bound cover, but my name at the very bottom is still easy to read. This was my Bible from grade school through my college years.

In graduate school I dabbled in a few modern translations, more out of novelty than conviction or heartfelt allegiance. When I came to teach at Wheaton College, I providentially came under the sway of people who used the Revised Standard Version in the form of the *Harper Study Bible*. It was one of the best things that ever happened to me. I used the *Harper Study Bible* with complete profit and delight until the appearance of the English Standard Version in 2001.

As my thumbnail autobiographical sketch implies, I do not believe that the King James Bible is the best translation for a reader today. One reason for this is that the KJV is not based on the best available knowledge about the Bible in its original Hebrew and Greek. Some parts of the KJV are based on ancient manuscripts that a majority of scholars today regard as inferior. I need to add, though, that in the past I have too glibly pronounced the KJV suspect in accuracy. It is not as accurate as modern translations that are based on the principle of essentially literal translation. But when set beside modern dynamic equivalent translations, the KJV is, on balance, more accurate as a rendition of what the original authors wrote.

The real case against the KJV for regular use today is the archaism of the language. For modern readers unfamiliar with the King James Bible, the language is an insurmountable barrier. Even for people who have always used the KJV, some of its words are a mystery.

But I need to say one more thing. Whenever I hear a modern colloquializing Bible read in public, I invariably feel the text to be flat and lacking in affective power. On such occasions I am dismayed that a segment of the Christian public has settled for something so inferior when better options exist. If I were forced to choose between the King James Bible and a modern colloquial translation, I would choose the KJV.

The history that I have just sketched would not by itself have equipped me to write a book on the King James Bible. The process that has eventuated in my present book began in 1978 with the appearance of the New International Version. I had been given an NIV New Testament when it appeared in advance of the complete Bible. It struck me as an insipid and lifeless translation, but I never analyzed why it struck me that way until I was asked to write the review of "the literary merits of the NIV" for *Christianity Today*. I subjected the NIV to literary analysis and came up with reasons why I think the NIV is an inferior translation. Having gone to that scholarly effort, I composed a lecture on the King James Bible for my course in sixteenth-century English literature. The principles that I articulated in that lecture form the basis for this book.

Why do we need another book on the King James Bible? The reasons are multiple. One is corrective in nature. In a day when debunking the Bible is common in academic circles, a lot of what is disseminated is simply incorrect. Additionally, as I implied above, the "sneer factor" is very strong in some circles. Some people imply by name-calling that the KJV is ridiculous, but the case for its inferiority is never laid out. I hope that in making the case for the King James Bible I will prompt people to see that the allegations against the KJV are rarely supported by honest argument.

Something parallel can happen among enthusiasts for the King James Bible. They, too, are capable of asserting their attitude toward the KJV without providing arguments and proofs for what makes the King James Bible excellent. I believe that readers of my book will see reasons for the claims that are made in favor of the King James Bible. A lot of the adulation surrounding the KJV on its four hundredth anniversary can be labeled propagandistic. My book will put the claims on a sound footing.

For the most part, the material that I cover in this book has been familiar to me for a long time. I have written multiple books on the history and principles of Bible translation. In addition, my own education and professional expertise lie in English literature, especially of the sixteenth and seventeenth centuries. I have had a longstanding interest in the Bible as literature and as a literary influence on English and American authors.

From the beginning, this book was designed to fall into two halves. The first half deals with the King James Bible in its original context and as an influence on Bible translation and culture since then. The second half of the book is literary in emphasis. This includes the King James Bible *as* literature—an analysis of its literary qualities—and the influence of the KJV on English and American literature.

The organization of the book will be further clarified when I say that it explores four spheres in which we can see the stature of the KJV:

1. Its status as the climax of a whole century of English Bible translation

2. Its influence in the subsequent history of Bible translation and in English-speaking culture
3. The literary excellence of the King James Bible itself
4. The influence of the King James Bible on English and American literature

In composing this book, I have adopted the stance of *telling the story* of the King James Bible—the story of how it came to be, the story of what kind of book it is, the story of how it influenced subsequent Bible translation and English and American culture, and the story of its literary qualities and literary influence.

For my King James text, I have used a reprint of the 1611 King James Bible published by Hendrickson Publishers in 2008. I have modernized spelling and sometimes punctuation for the sake of readability but have preserved archaic pronouns and verb endings. When quoting extended passages of prose I have used a paragraph format instead of the verse-by-verse indentation of the KJV.

Credit for the idea of this book goes to Lane Dennis, president of Crossway. I also hereby record my heartfelt gratitude to the interlibrary loan staff of Buswell Library on the campus of Wheaton College; they were exemplary colleagues in being always helpful and never complaining, and I could not have written this book without their assistance.

ABBREVIATIONS OF BIBLE TRANSLATIONS

CEV	Contemporary English Version
ESV	English Standard Version
GNB	Good News Bible
HCSB	Holman Christian Standard Bible
KJV	King James Version
MESSAGE	*The Message*
NASB	New American Standard Bible
NCV	New Century Version
NEB	New English Bible
NIV	New International Version
NKJV	New King James Bible
NLT	New Living Translation
RSV	Revised Standard Version

PART ONE

The King James Bible
in Its Own Day

1

IN THE BEGINNING

I had no man to imitate, neither was helped with English of any that had interpreted the same or such like thing in the Scripture beforetime.

—WILLIAM TYNDALE, commenting on his task
as translator of the Bible into English

WHAT IS THE ACTUAL ORIGIN of the King James Bible? Surely its lineage needs to be traced backward from the committee that assembled to begin its deliberations in 1604. But how far back must we go to find the origins of the King James Version?

Let us consider an analogy: what is the origin of modern jet air travel? We might trace it back to the first jet airplane. Or we might trace it back to propeller airplanes of the 1940s as representing the forerunner of improved jet engineering. But neither of those would represent the situation accurately. The origin of modern jet airplanes is ultimately the Wright brothers' rudimentary aircraft flown at Kitty Hawk in 1903. Before the history of flight could unfold, someone needed to master the essential principles of flight and prove that flying could be done.

John Wycliffe

The ultimate origin of English Bible translation is the work of John Wycliffe (ca. 1320–1384) and his associates. A towering theologian of his day, the Oxford-educated Wycliffe is known as "the morning star of the Reformation." Although Wycliffe began his clerical life within the Catholic Church, his outspoken criticism of corruption in the church and his radical political ideas eventually led church officials to pronounce his teachings heretical.

A "fact sheet" on what is the Wycliffite version of the Bible (so-called because it was the product of Wycliffe's associates more than of him) is as follows:

- The English of the translation is Middle English (the language of Chaucer), not modern English.
- Over 150 copies of the Wycliffite Bible still exist, and they are all in handwritten form because the Wycliffite Bible predated the invention of the printing press.
- The text of the Bible from which the translation was made is the Latin Vulgate.
- The Wycliffite Bible exists in two versions. The first is a literal translation of the Latin Vulgate text. The second has an eye on the English "receptor language" and is accordingly more understandable by an English audience.
- The first complete Bibles in the two translations appeared around 1380–1384. There were no *printed* versions of the Wycliffite Bible until 1731 (New Testament), and the standard printed edition was published in Oxford in 1850.
- Even though the Wycliffite Bible circulated in handwritten manuscripts, only the rich could afford to own a copy, with the result that the greatest circulation consisted of oral readings from the Bible by traveling preachers known as Lollards (many of whom were burned as heretics by the church establishment).

"The Wycliffe Bible was . . . not merely a book but an event. There attaches to it . . . a historical as well as a literary importance. For while it announces that a new stage has been reached in the evolution of our native tongue, it marks . . . a momentous epoch in our religious development." —H. W. Hamilton-Hoare, *The Evolution of the English Bible*

What the King James Bible Owes to Wycliffe

In what sense can the Wycliffite Bible be considered the ultimate origin of the KJV? First, whoever does something *first* is in some sense the originator of that thing. Someone had to have the vision for an English translation of the Bible before it could become an established institution in the English-speaking world. Wycliffe and his associates had that vision and proved that the vision could be put into practice.

Second, from the beginning, the impetus behind English Bible translation has been spiritual and evangelical. To translate the Bible is qualitatively different in its purpose from translating Homer or Plato. Further, the goal is that laypeople might understand the message of the Bible and obey it in their lives. Wycliffe's associate John Purvey wrote that the goal of his translation was that through it God might "grant to us all grace to know well and to keep well holy writ."[1] Elsewhere we read that the purpose was "to save all men in our realm whom God will have saved."[2] This will be a theme through the whole subsequent history of English Bible translation, including the King James Bible.

Finally, the Wycliffite translators eventually evolved the principle that the language and syntax of an English translation must be clear and understandable to an English reader. In the words of the prologue to the second Wycliffite translation, the translators aimed "to translate after the meaning and not only after the words."[3] This is not an endorsement of the practice of modern dynamic equivalence to change details of the original biblical text into something equivalent in modern life. Instead it is a comment against transposing Latin syntax and vocabulary into English.

William Tyndale

Important as John Wycliffe is to the early history of English Bible translation, William Tyndale (1494–1536) is the person who deserves highest homage as the fountainhead of English Bible translation. I have told his story in multiple places elsewhere, but my emphasis this time is different. In keeping with the focus of this book, I am interested in what Tyndale contributed to the King James Bible.

Tyndale shares something important with Wycliffe and the Lollards that he does not share with the King James translators: he translated the Bible under threat to his life. Eventually he died a martyr because of his translation of the Bible. Educated at Oxford as Wycliffe was, Tyndale was a linguistic genius whose expertise in seven languages dazzled the scholarly world of his

---

Important Dates in William Tyndale's Life as a Translator

1512	Tyndale graduates from Oxford University with a BA (MA in 1515).
1516	Erasmus's improved Greek New Testament is published, providing a superior original text from which Tyndale can work.
1521	Tyndale is ordained to the priesthood, the same year in which Cardinal Wolsey oversees the burning of "heretical" Reformation books at St. Paul's Cathedral.
1524	Tyndale relocates to Germany to translate the New Testament in hiding.
1525	Tyndale's New Testament is published.
1526	Copies of the New Testament arrive in England, smuggled in bales of wool and bags of wheat. Catholic bishops burn as many copies as they can confiscate.
1530	Tyndale's English translation of the Pentateuch is published.
1534	Tyndale's revised New Testament is printed.
1535	Tyndale is lured out of hiding by a Catholic sympathizer, imprisoned, and declared a heretic.
1536	Tyndale is strangled and burned at the stake near Brussels in Belgium.

day. Early in his scholarly and clerical life he came to view the translation of the Bible into English as his life calling, and since he shared Wycliffe's Reformation ideas regarding the church, he quickly found himself an opposed and then hunted man.

Tyndale's goal was the same as Wycliffe's—to see the Bible infiltrate the whole cross section of his country. In particular, Tyndale wanted laypeople to have access to the Bible in their own language. He famously told a Catholic that he aspired to "cause a boy that driveth the plough" to "know more of the Scripture than thou dost." The reference to the plowboy has been extravagantly misinterpreted. It is not a comment on Tyndale's preferred English style but rather a statement about (a) how widely Tyndale wanted the Bible distributed across the English social strata and (b) the large quantity of the Bible that Tyndale wanted people to know—"more of the Scripture" than just the passages doled out in mass and church services.

How Tyndale Started a Social Climate That Paved the Way for the KJV

Early translators and disseminators of the English Bible were opposed and sometimes murdered by Catholic Church officials and their henchmen. But by the time the King James translators did their work, the situation was completely reversed. That translation was actually instigated by the monarch, King James I. The teams of translators met in the three most prestigious locations imaginable—Oxford and Cambridge Universities and the Jerusalem room just off the entrance to Westminster Abbey in London. The work of the committee was accompanied by fanfare and had full sanction of the Church of England. How could this have happened?

The answer is that the work of Wycliffe and Tyndale started a grassroots revolution in England. The Bible, by its own testimony, is "living and active" (Heb. 4:12, ESV). Once laypeople in England had their appetite for the Bible whetted, there was no stopping the movement of English Bible translation. In Wycliffe's day, when the Bible was available only in handwritten form,

25

townspeople flocked to hear parts of the Bible read orally by traveling preachers known as Lollards. Even though this was an underground movement, it flourished. Only the rich could afford to buy the expensive volumes, but farmers were willing to rent a copy by the day for the price of a load of hay.[4]

The populist hunger for the Word was even more evident once Tyndale's New Testament made it from the Continent to England. Just at the time of the printing of Tyndale's New Testament, governmental officials had banned ships from Germany from entering English ports. But catastrophic rains so devastated the sowing season in England that the ban was lifted. Copies of Tyndale's New Testament were smuggled into England in sacks of flour and bales of cloth. Even though an act of synod known as the Constitutions of Oxford (1409) had long since made it illegal for anyone to translate or even read any part of the Bible in the English vernacular, copies nonetheless flooded England. At one point Cuthbert Tunstall, Bishop of London, bought a large stock of copies of Tyndale's New Testament and burned them at St. Paul's Cathedral, but the whole enterprise was a trick orchestrated by a sympathizer of Tyndale. The money gained from the sale of the Bibles actually gave Tyndale the capital he needed to pay off printing debts and begin a new round of publication.

> "There is no shortage of evidence of the gatherings of people of all ages, all over the country, to read and hear these English Scriptures [as translated by Tyndale]—and reading meant, so often, reading aloud. . . . The corner that English readers turned in the 1530s, stepping into direct access to the whole Bible, did not lead to one or two curious Bible effects. . . . On the contrary: turning that corner was suddenly to be faced with a vast, rich, sunlit territory." —David Daniell, *The Bible in English*

There is another aspect of the social revolution that Tyndale effected that is often overlooked. Up to the time of Tyndale, virtually all important scholarly and ecclesiastical discourse in Europe was conducted in Latin. Even the official church Bible, the

Vulgate, was a Latin document. It was just assumed that the really important intellectual matters would be conducted in Latin.

If the idea of an English Bible had become mainstream by the time the King James translators sat around the table to begin translating the Bible, it was a result of what Tyndale had accomplished nearly a century earlier. Tyndale's Bible ended the hegemony that Latin had enjoyed in the church and academy for centuries, and it struck a blow for the vernacular in all spheres of English society. One scholar theorizes that "the real horror" of Tyndale's New Testament to the church officials "was not so much the words in themselves . . . but that they were English words."[5]

Yet another detail that we need to note is that whereas Wycliffe had translated the Bible into Middle English, by Tyndale's time modern English had begun. In this way, too, Tyndale is the fountain from which all subsequent English Bible translation flowed. Additionally, the specific kind of English that Tyndale helped to establish and then perpetuate as his translation continued to be read is important. David Daniell calls it an English plain style.[6] This should not be construed to mean colloquial, as in everyday conversation or in the mode of modern colloquial Bible translations. It means Anglo-Saxon words as opposed to Latin-derived words—plain in the sense of clear. This is a plain style in the mode of Shakespeare's plays, as articulated in the cliché "without Tyndale, no Shakespeare."

The Principles of Translation That Tyndale Bequeathed to the KJV

In addition to initiating a hunger for the vernacular Bible among English laypeople, Tyndale formulated and then put into practice the principles of English Bible translation that the King James translators also followed. Tyndale knew that he was a pioneer and that what he was doing would be influential to posterity (as in fact it has been). Despite that, Tyndale left no detailed explanation of his philosophy of translation, not even in his preface to the New Testament, which is instead a statement of evangelical doctrine and of Tyndale's desire that people be saved. Nonetheless it is relatively easy to infer Tyndale's philosophy of translation, which was fully embraced by the King James translators.

"The accuracy and easy-to-read-style of the King James Version of 1611 dwarfed the work of all previous translations. And yet, the work of William Tyndale should be valued as the greatest influence on English translations and its language. . . . Even the famous translators of the 1611 King James Version relied heavily upon the work of Tyndale." —Donald L. Brake, *A Visual History of the English Bible*

Tyndale's first principle was that an English translation of the Bible needs to start with the words of the original Hebrew and Greek of the Old and New Testaments, respectively. This may seem obvious to us, but it was not obvious before Tyndale's time. The Latin Vulgate had been the assumed starting point for serious Bible study and translation for centuries. Even Wycliffe and his associates had no viable alternative but to start with the Latin translation of the original Hebrew and Greek texts. So far as professional expertise was concerned, Tyndale was above all a linguist, though of course he was secondarily a theologian.

A second principle that we can discern in Tyndale is fidelity to the actual words of the original text. In fact, Tyndale's commitment to preserving the very words of the original was so strong that he actually invented new English words to reproduce the very words of the Hebrew and Greek original—words like *intercession*, *atonement*, and *passover*. We will see that the King James translators went even further than Tyndale in making sure that they translated exactly what was in the original, but the essential pattern had been laid by Tyndale.

A third principle that we can discern in Tyndale's actual translation is that Tyndale expected his readers to rise to what is called standard formal English. Two things have obscured this and skewed modern thinking on the subject. One is Tyndale's famous comment about the plowboy, which is a comment not on style (as it is commonly misinterpreted to be) but on how widely and deeply Tyndale wanted biblical knowledge to permeate the minds of individual people. Second, there are a few famous colloquialisms in Tyndale, as when the Serpent tells Eve, "Tush, ye shall not die," or when Joseph is called "a luckie felowe." But these are anomalies in Tyndale's Bible. As much as 80 percent of Tyndale's translation was carried over into the comparable parts of the King James Bible. The KJV, in turn, is often considered the very touchstone of eloquence, so the claim of modern colloquial Bible translators that Tyndale is their model cannot possibly be true.

Summary

The King James Bible did not suddenly appear in 1611. In a significant way it had been in the making for over two centuries. Furthermore, William Tyndale is not the head of the river of Renaissance Bible translation. Some of the famous phrases that found their way into the KJV first appeared in the Wycliffite Bible. Nonetheless, William Tyndale is the forerunner to whom the King James Bible owes the most.

Further Reading

H. W. Hamilton-Hoare, *The Evolution of the English Bible* (1901).

James Baikie, *The English Bible and Its Story* (1928).

Benson Bobrick, *Wide as the Waters: The Story of the English Bible and the Revolution It Inspired* (2001).

Brian Moynahan, *God's Bestseller: William Tyndale, Thomas More, and the Writing of the English Bible* (2002).

David Daniell, *The Bible in English: Its History and Influence* (2003).

2

FROM TYNDALE
TO THE KING JAMES BIBLE

*Truly (good Christian reader) we never thought from the begin-
ning, that we should need to make a new translation, nor yet to
make of a bad one a good one, . . . but to make a good one better,
or out of many good ones, one principal good one.*

—"The Translators to the Reader," King James Version

THE INFLUENCE OF WILLIAM TYNDALE on the King James
translators has been so aggressively urged by some that the impression is sometimes given that the lineage can be traced without
intermediary from Tyndale to the King James Version. This is
not the true history of the matter, however. The contributions of
a succession of translations between Tyndale and the KJV are as
important to the King James Bible as the contributions of Tyndale.
After all, Tyndale translated only about half of the Bible.

The purpose of this chapter is to sketch the major English
Bible translations between Tyndale and the KJV, with emphasis
on what these translations contributed to the King James Bible.

To give my discussion a focus, I propose to answer the following three questions:

1. The preface to the KJV makes it clear that the translators had endeavored to produce the best possible translation "from many good ones." What are these good translations that became woven into the KJV, and what were their specific contributions?

2. Tyndale lived in hiding and was murdered for translating the Bible, whereas the King James translators were an honored group as they translated the Bible. What forces arrived on the scene that might explain such a drastic turnaround?

3. The King James Bible is an anomaly in carrying the name of a British monarch. Is there something in the history of English Bible translation that might account for this situation?

Quick Overview of Translation Dates and Names	
1535	Coverdale's Bible
1537	Matthew's Bible
1539	Great Bible
1560	Geneva Bible
1568	Bishops' Bible
1611	King James Bible

Two Immediate Successors to Tyndale

Tyndale translated the New Testament, the Pentateuch, and a large part of the Old Testament historical books before he was imprisoned in 1535. But the ferment in Protestant translation of the Bible was so intense that the first complete English Bible appeared in print while Tyndale was still alive, and a second the year after his death. The first complete English Bible was produced by Miles Coverdale, who had served as an assistant to William Tyndale.

Coverdale's Bible

Despite Coverdale's association with Tyndale, the two were in some ways opposites. Tyndale was rigorous in working from the original Hebrew and Greek texts, while Coverdale did not read Hebrew and Greek. As a result, Tyndale's penchant for accuracy, even if it produced awkward constructions, gave way in Coverdale's Bible to an aesthetic flair and feel for stylistic smoothness. We can compare, for example, these three versions of Exodus 2:1–2 in their original spelling:

- *Tyndale.* And there went a man of the house of Leui and toke a doughter of Leui. And the wife conceaued and bare sonne. And whe she saw that it was a proper childe, she hyd him thre monthes longe.
- *Coverdale.* And there wente forth a man of the house of Leui, and toke a doughter of Leui. And the wife conceaued and bare a sonne. And whan she sawe y it was a proper childe, she hyd him thre monethes.
- *King James.* And there went a man of the house of Leui, and tooke to wife a daughter of Leui. And the woman conceiued, and bare a sonne: and when see saw him that he was a goodly childe, shee hid him three moneths.

We can see that Coverdale's rendering flows more smoothly than Tyndale's, and additionally that the KJV adds improving touches to Coverdale. Coverdale's translation of the Psalms was so stylistically accomplished that it became the standard Psalter for many years and was used in the Book of Common Prayer.

Second, whereas Tyndale was an uncompromising Reformer who alienated both church and state officials, Coverdale moved with ease among people with whom he did not totally agree. As a result, he lived to the age of eighty-one and worked on two subsequent English Bible translations. Coverdale courted the favor of King Henry VIII in regard to his translation, and the second edition of his translation (1537) was published with this endorsement on the title page: "Set forth with the King's most gracious license."

Throughout the sixteenth century, the printing of Bibles was very closely tied to the religious leanings of the ruling monarch. Before Tyndale had begun his work, Henry VIII had promised the pope that he would burn any "untrue translations" of the Bible, so the Bible was suppressed.[1] But by the time of Coverdale's Bible, Henry declared, "If there be no heresies [in it], then in God's name let it go abroad among our people," whereupon it was put into circulation.[2] All of this helps to explain Tyndale's otherwise enigmatic dying words: "Lord, open the king of England's eyes."

When Coverdale's Bible received the king's imprimatur, a whole new era of English Bible translation arrived. The hated Constitutions of Oxford, which had forbidden English people to read or own even a scrap of a vernacular Bible, were now abolished. Some copies of Coverdale's Bible became the first of the famous chained Bibles—Bibles chained to a desk in English cathedrals or parish churches, where people were free to read them. Possibly the greatest influence of Coverdale lies in the fact that his rendition of the Psalms "remains intact, with all its mistakes and all its beauty, in the Prayer Book version."[3]

Matthew's Bible

Thomas Matthew was the pen name or pseudonym of John Rogers. Like Tyndale, he was a Reformer who was martyred for his Protestant faith. Rogers met his death as a "Smithfield martyr" when the Catholic Queen Mary came to throne. The year 1537 saw the publication of both the second edition of Coverdale's Bible and the first publication of Matthew's Bible, and both received the king's licensure. Matthew's Bible is a conflation of the translations of Tyndale and Coverdale.

In an era of censorship like the sixteenth century, for publishers everything depended on the conferring or withholding of official sanction. Thomas Cromwell, chief minister to King

Henry VIII and influential in ecclesiastical decisions, threw his weight behind Matthew's Bible. He encouraged bishops to order copies for their churches (of which there were nine thousand in England). Cromwell thus put into effect what he had proposed in a letter to the king—that the vernacular Bible "may be sold and read of every person, without danger of any act, proclamation, or ordinance heretofore granted to the contrary."[4]

Contributions of Coverdale and Rogers

Coverdale's and Matthew's Bibles between them introduced the following features into the flow of English Bible translation:

- Publication of whole Bibles
- Official "state" licensure, with the result that English Bibles circulated freely
- Ecclesiastical sanction in the form of making a Bible available to the public in cathedrals and parish churches
- Chapter summaries and marginal notes
- Division of the material into chapters and paragraphs (but not verses)
- Inclusion of scholarly notes and cross references, thereby producing a rudimentary study Bible

---

Two Ecclesiastical Translations

Coverdale's and Matthew's Bibles are a natural pair by virtue of their (a) belonging to the Tyndale tradition, (b) appearing in close chronological proximity, and (c) turning the tide from the English Bible as a forbidden book to an officially licensed book. The Great Bible (1539) and Bishops' Bible (1568), though separated from each other by three decades, are also a natural pair by virtue of being translations produced by clerics under the institutional oversight of Church of England officials.

The Great Bible

Once the English Bible had gained official acceptance, sentiment grew for the production of a single, definitive translation for use in the church. As early as 1534, Archbishop Thomas Cranmer had attempted and failed to secure support for an official translation done by bishops. When Matthew's Bible appeared in 1537, Cranmer tipped his hand in favor of this translation. Thomas Cromwell, minister to the king, thereupon enlisted Coverdale to undertake a light revision of Matthew's Bible with the intention that it would become the standard Bible for the Church of England. The revised version of the Great Bible (1540), sometimes called "Cranmer's Bible," became that Bible.

What was it like to live in England when the English Bible ceased to be a suppressed book? An early biographer of Thomas Cranmer painted this picture:

"It was wonderful to see with what joy the book of God was received, not only among the learneder sort and those that were noted for lovers of the reformation, but generally all England over among all the vulgar and common people; with what greediness God's word was read, and what resort to places where the reading of it was. Everybody that could bought the book and busily read it; or got others to read it to them, if they could not themselves; and diverse among the elderly learned to read on purpose. And even little boys flocked among the rest to hear portions of the Holy Scriptures read." —John Strype, *Memorials of the Most Reverend Father in God Thomas Cranmer*

The title Great Bible is not honorific but instead denotes the immense physical size of the book. The king's decree regarding the translation correctly labeled it "the largest and greatest volume, to be had in every church."[5] One of the two most important things about the Great Bible is hinted in a statement appearing on the title page: "This is the Bible appointed to the use of the churches." It was the official Bible for the Church of England.

In keeping with that, the Great Bible became another of the famed chained Bibles in English churches, placed in "some convenient place" within churches throughout England. Bishop

Edmund Bonner of London placed six chained Bibles in St. Paul's Cathedral. Although the initial instructions had stipulated that the Bibles were to be read "without disputations," people actually crowded around the Bible and engaged in arguments, even during church services. Further rules eventually forbade reading of the Bibles during church services.

The second important feature of the Great Bible is that it became the basis of the scriptural passages in the 1549 Book of Common Prayer. Subsequent versions of the Anglican Prayer Book likewise drew upon the Great Bible.

The Bishops' Bible

The desire for a uniform and therefore "controlled" English Bible continued to percolate. The movement acquired new impetus with the accession of Queen Elizabeth I in 1557. Probably the inciting force for the queen's interest in a new church Bible was the instant success of the Puritan Geneva Bible, published in 1560. It included radical Protestant sentiment in its marginal notes, as well as Calvinistic preferences in translation. And to make matters worse, the inferiority of the Great Bible to the new Geneva Bible was obvious.

The failed attempt of 1534 to mobilize the bishops to undertake an official church Bible was revived in 1563. Archbishop Matthew Parker was in charge of the venture. The directive was to use the Great Bible as the starting point and to deviate from it only where it was deemed inaccurate. Published in 1568, the Bishops' Bible was another lavish production in its physical format.

The resulting Bishops' Bible proved to be a paradoxical experiment. Even though Queen Elizabeth initiated the move to produce this new translation, and although the title page carried a large portrait of the queen, the queen never officially endorsed the Bishops' Bible. The church hierarchy attempted to force the use of the new translation (a copy was required to be in every cathedral, church, and home of every archbishop and bishop), but the translation never caught on with a public that could use

A Natural Evolution

Literary scholar John Livingston Lowes once wrote the following about the relation of the King James Bible to the preceding century of Bible translation: "The 'Authorized Version' represents a slow, almost impersonal evolution. For it is, in reality, itself a revision, resting upon earlier versions, and these, in turn, depend in varying degrees upon each other, so that through the gradual exercise of something which approaches natural selection, there has come about, in both diction and phraseology, a true survival of the fittest. . . . The long process of version upon version served (to use Dante's phrase) as 'a sieve for noble words.'" One way to see this is to collect some famous words and phrases that various translations added to the process of refinement that culminated in the KJV.

Wycliffe Bible: *first fruits, strait gate, peradventure, son of perdition, enter thou into the joy of thy Lord, the deep things of God.*

Tyndale's Bible: *be not weary in well doing; my brother's keeper; the salt of the earth; the signs of the times; a law unto themselves; the spirit is willing, but the flesh is weak; fight the good fight; with God all things are possible; the patience of Job; an eye for an eye; O ye of little faith; he went out . . . and wept bitterly; give us this day our daily bread; in him we live and move and have our being.*

Coverdale: *the valley of the shadow of death; thou anointest my head with oil; baptized into his death; tender mercies; loving-kindness; respect of persons; even, neither,* and *yea* to introduce a Hebrew parallelism.

Geneva: *smite them hip and thigh; vanity of vanities; my cup runneth over; except a man be born again; comfort ye, comfort ye my people.*

whatever translation they preferred. The lavish Bishops' Bible had external impressiveness on its side, but the simple and small Geneva Bible easily outstripped it with the Bible-reading public. The greatest shock remains to be stated. Even though the Geneva Bible was the best translation on the scene at the end of the sixteenth century, the Bishops' Bible was the stipulated starting point for the King James translators!

The Geneva Bible

The case can be made that the most successful English Bible before the King James Bible was the Puritan-generated Geneva Bible. Even though the King James translators started with the Bishops' Bible, in my experience the Geneva Bible seems closer to the KJV than the other sixteenth-century predecessors, including Tyndale.

As the title suggests, the Geneva Bible was produced in Calvin's Geneva after the Catholic Queen Mary acceded to the English throne in 1553. The work was performed anonymously. The Puritan aspect of the translation comes out most clearly in the commentary that appears in the margins of the book. These are not simply scholarly textual notes but sometimes interpretive and polemical notes on theological and political matters. The superior accuracy of the Geneva translations over other sixteenth-century translations is a matter of scholarly consensus. But what propelled the Geneva Bible to the forefront were certain printing innovations (see list below).

The Geneva Bible was "the King James Bible" of its day. It proved that before an English Bible can be successful, it needs to win the minds and hearts of its readers. Official endorsement does not produce an influential English Bible. Excellence of form and content does. Whereas Tyndale's translation, while excellent, strikes a modern reader as archaic and rough in its flow, the Geneva Bible (available in modern facsimile reprint) is surprisingly easy to read.

The Geneva Bible eventually gave way to the King James Bible, but it was a great forerunner. It was the Bible most used

---

Innovations in the Geneva Bible

- Small size, making it portable and affordable, and giving it mass appeal instead of mere church or state sanction
- Division of the text into numbered verses
- Readable roman typeface instead of the difficult-to-read black gothic lettering used in other translations
- Italics for words added by the translators, to make the text understandable in English, but not present in the original text
- Inclusion of interpretive notes and prefaces to books of the Bible, making it a rudimentary study Bible

---

by Shakespeare and carried to America on the *Mayflower*. It was for fifty years the household Bible of English-speaking evangelicals. Considering that Tyndale translated only half of the Bible, it is likely that "in the lineage of the King James Bible this volume is by all means the most important single volume."[6]

Summary

The three questions posed at the beginning of this chapter have received the following answers: (1) The "many good" translations that the King James translators used to forge "one principal good one" are the ones surveyed in this chapter. (2) English Bible translation ceased to be a forbidden activity when church and state authorities lent their sanction to it. If Tyndale could have survived a year or two longer, he might have returned to England as a hailed scholar. (3) Beginning with Coverdale's and Matthew's Bibles, English monarchs exercised final authority on what translations of the Bible might be published and circulated, so the role that King James I played in the translation that bears his name is not unusual.

Further Reading

Samuel McComb, *The Making of the English Bible* (1909); the best source on the felicitous phrases that various translations added.

F. F. Bruce, *History of the Bible in English* (1978).

Alister McGrath, *In the Beginning: The Story of the King James Bible and How It Changed a Nation, a Language, and a Culture* (2001).

Donald L. Brake, *A Visual History of the English Bible: The Tumultuous Tale of the World's Bestselling Book* (2008).

3

THE MAKING
OF THE KING JAMES BIBLE

In respect of both equipment and method, . . . the translation was made according to the highest standards of scholarship and the most advanced knowledge of the day.

—GEDDES MACGREGOR, *The Bible in the Making*

WHEN WE CELEBRATE THE BIRTHDAY of a loved one, our thoughts usually turn to the circumstances of his or her birth. Where did the birth occur? On what day? At what hospital or clinic? To what kind of home did the infant go upon release from the hospital? What were the early days at home like?

The four hundredth anniversary of the publication of the King James Bible is a time when we naturally want to know the story of its beginnings. That story has fascinated scholars so much that it has been told many times and with surprising frequency in recent times.[1] Yet the average person does not know the story.

I will provide a short biography of one of the greatest and most influential books in the history of the world. The purpose of the present chapter is to tell the story of the *process* by which the King James Bible came into existence and lived its early life. The next chapter will explore the *product* that resulted from that process, namely, the King James Bible of 1611. In order to give a focus to my account of origins and early reception, I will organize the story around the following five questions:

1. Who came up with the idea for the King James Bible?
2. Who did the translation?
3. What was the process of translation like?
4. What were the circumstances of the first appearance of the King James Version as a printed book?
5. What was the early history of the book's reception?

The Project Is Conceived

The idea for a new translation of the Bible was conceived in an instant at a famous event of English history. The place was Hampton Court, a royal palace dating from the reign of King Henry VIII, located on the bank of the Thames River in the London suburb of Hampton. The occasion was the notorious Hampton Court Conference of 1604.

The circumstances of that conference were as follows. Queen Elizabeth I died in 1603 after reigning as monarch for nearly half a century. She was succeeded by the Scottish King James I. The Elizabethan Compromise (also called the Elizabethan Settlement) between Protestant doctrine and Catholic ecclesiology and worship had been under serious attack for a long time from the sizeable Puritan contingent in England. In 1590, as King of Scotland, James had cast scorn on high-church Anglicanism with his verdict that the Church of England "is an ill-mumbled Mass in English."[2]

This gave the Puritans hope that James was actually one of them, so as the procession of James wound its way southward from Scotland to London, a group of Puritan leaders intercepted the king with a "Millenary Petition" (so-called because it purported to be the product of a thousand Anglican clergy with

Puritan leanings) requesting a diminishment of the Catholic trappings of the Church of England. This petition eventuated in the Hampton Court Conference held January 14, 16, and 18 in 1604. While James might have had sympathies with the Puritans on some religious matters, he unveiled an extreme devotion to an old doctrine called the Divine Right of Kings to rule as they please. The conference turned out to be a farce, designed by James to vent his anger against the Puritans for their democratic political leanings. All of the Puritan requests were summarily dismissed. At the end of one of his tirades the king threatened the Puritans with the announcement that they had better conform to the Church of England "or else I will harry them out of the land or worse." With everything seemingly lost to the Puritan leaders assembled, a last-minute request was made for a new translation of the English Bible. The preface to the King James Bible provides this narrative of the event:

> . . . upon the importunate petitions of the Puritans at his Majesty's coming to this Crown, the Conference at Hampton Court having been appointed for hearing their complaints, when by force of reason they were put from all other grounds, they had recourse at the last to this shift, that they could not with good conscience subscribe to the Communion book, since it maintained the Bible as it was there translated, which was, as they said, a most corrupted translation. And although this was judged to be but a very poor and empty shift, yet even here upon did his Majesty begin to bethink himself of the good that might ensue by a new translation, and presently after gave order for this translation which is now presented unto thee.

I have quoted this passage to convey something of the inauspicious atmosphere in which the King James Bible was conceptualized.

The statement from the preface tells only half of the story. An attendee at the conference fills in the details.[3] The high-church Bishop Richard Bancroft belittled the Puritan request for a new translation with the snide put-down that "if every man's humor should be followed, there would be no end of translating." The bishop's sarcasm backfired, though, because he did not know that the king was already inclined toward a new translation. The king replied to Bancroft that he "wished that some special pains should be taken in that behalf for one uniform translation (professing that he could never yet see a Bible well translated in English, but the worst of all his Majesty thought the Geneva to be)."

So this was the origin of the King James Bible—a "poor and empty" request from a handful of dejected Puritans, granted by the king as a sneer directed to the Puritans' favorite Bible and accompanied by a denigration of the whole tradition of English Bible translation. It is hard to imagine a less auspicious origin for the mighty King James Bible.

Several mysteries and contradictions surround the origin of the King James Bible. Here are four of them:

1. Why did the Puritans ask for a new translation of the Bible when their preferred Bible—the Genevan—was the well-established best seller of its day?

2. Why did a profane king throw his weight behind such a spiritual venture as a new Bible translation?

3. Why did the Puritans continue to prefer the Geneva Bible of 1560 over the new 1611 Bible that their leaders had requested?

4. Since the Bishops' Bible was not the best English Bible in circulation in 1604, why was it chosen as the starting point for the new translation?

Who Were the Translators?

More surprises greet us as we proceed to ask who were chosen for the task of translating. The first surprise is the size of the translation team. Although Richard Bancroft, Bishop of London and overseer of the project under King James, wrote in 1604 that the king had approved fifty-four men to work on the translation, surviving lists indicate that forty-seven scholars actually did the work. This is a staggering number of translators for what was, after all, a revision of an existing Bible, not a new translation.

Furthermore, the translators were divided into six committees, again a number that might easily prove unworkable. These six committees met at three different locations, two each at Westminster Abbey in London and the Universities of Oxford and Cambridge. A further thing that we know about the translators is that they were people who were dedicated to the project and who undertook the work at a sacrifice to themselves (and surely to their families if they were married). I note in passing that the translators were very modestly paid.

Then when we look at institutional affiliations of the translators, and further at their known theological leanings, the picture gets even more unlikely. The list of personnel was a triumph of compromise and balance. The Hampton Court Conference had been an explosion of high-handed discrimination against the Puritan faction of the Church of England (four handpicked Puritan moderates were set against eighteen Church of England adversaries).[4] Yet in choosing the translators Bishop Bancroft and King James rose above a partisan spirit, as did the translators in their deliberations. In a spirit of fair-mindedness, all sides of the Church of England were represented, from Puritans to extreme high churchmen to various grades between those poles. Approximately a fourth of the group were Puritan in their convictions.[5]

We get still more evidence of a delicate balancing act when we tease out the meanings of the three locations chosen for the meetings of the committees. Here is how Benson Bobrick sizes up the situation:

> By tradition, Oxford was associated for the most part with High Church and royalist sentiments; Cambridge with dissidents—reformers, martyrs, and exiles. Both were also, strictly speaking, secular institutions. Westminster, on the other hand, represented the clerical and legal aspects of the venture, for all the officials of the abbey were appointed by the sovereign, making it a sort of Cathedral of the Crown.[6]

Four Surprises in the Choice of Translators

1. Even though the project was born in a spirit of religious and political contentiousness, the translators were not chosen on the basis of their religious leanings (other than that all were members of the Church of England). All factions of the English religious scene were well represented.

2. The translators were chosen solely on the basis of their scholarly ability, and the list is a roll call of the best scholars in Hebrew, Greek, and biblical knowledge. Given the religious contentiousness of the times, it is surprising that the translators were chosen for scholarly ability rather than known religious viewpoint.

3. Even though the translators were chosen because of their scholarly and academic stature, all but one were also ordained members of the Church of England. In other words, the translators were not only scholars but also clerics.

4. Despite the worthiness of these scholars, they were very modestly paid, and (more importantly) raising the money to pay them was an ongoing battle among various parties (including the king and officials of the Church of England); the translators could hardly have avoided being embarrassed by the haggling over their pay.

It is hard to imagine a more carefully orchestrated game plan than this.

If all of the foregoing seems to add up to a story of fat-cat complacency, we have gotten the picture wrong. Eugene Peterson's depiction of the translators "working in the sumptuous furnishings of the great universities and the royal court" is preposterous.[7] None of the translation was done at court. Much of the work was done in individual offices or studies at college or church. As for the regular committee meetings, we all know what the meeting rooms of colleges and churches are like, and the word *sumptuous* is not an accurate descriptor.

One expert on the King James translators describes them as scholars who would

> sit down in a cold stone room by the fire and discuss in capable fashion the books of the Bible they were to translate. . . . Many of

them labored like monks in rooms so cold and damp, except close to the fires, that fingers and joints got stiff. . . . They worked at odd hours, early in the mornings and late at night, as other duties permitted. They endured rigors that we would think beyond us.[8]

Several modern books fill out the portraits of the translators,[9] who emerge as a very human lot—approximately the same as the committees that have produced our familiar modern translations. Most of the King James translators have entries in *The Dictionary of National Biography*, but they were not celebrities. Most of them worked hard for their scholarly or church livings, and one thing that they shared during the process of translation was an unusual capacity for work. Some of the translators were married, and some were single. They were middle-aged and were on average fifty years old—scholars in their prime.[10]

The Process of Translation

We know certain details of how the translators went about their work on the basis of two contemporaries who took notes on committee meetings that they attended. It would be satisfying to know more than we do. The following things are certain: the process was a communal rather than individualistic one (in contrast to the first English translations), and it was meticulous. The following data represents a consensus.[11]

First, the process of translation took approximately six years. The first two or three years were spent in haggling between church officials and the always financially strapped king about who would pay for the project. Individual translators began their study and translation during these years as well. Then another two or three years were spent in the official translation by individuals and committees. As the accompanying summary shows, the process by which all parts of the Bible moved through defined steps was systematic and thorough. It is nothing short of astounding that individual committees completed their work by the end of 1608, at which time the accumulated manuscript copies went to the

General Committee of Review. Starting in January 1609, this committee met for nine months in the Stationers' Hall in London.

Here is a slightly streamlined account of how the books of the Bible wound their way through the translation process:

1. Individual members of the six committees worked by themselves on a block of assigned biblical material.
2. These scholars met regularly with other team members; variations were negotiated, and eventually an agreed-upon version was codified.
3. When completed, books of the Bible were passed on to all the other committees for review. This means the entire Bible was perused by every translator.
4. Committees could send recommendations for change to the original committee, and if no agreement resulted, the disputed details would be saved for meetings of the leaders of the six committees.
5. There was always the option of submitting difficult questions to experts beyond the translation team.
6. Eventually the entire proposed Bible (an annotated and amended Bishops' Bible, in effect) was sent to the three translation heads, and this General Committee of Review, with members drawn from each committee, determined a single final version.

Among translators of the English Bible, only John Wycliffe and his associates and William Tyndale began without an existing English Bible in their language as their starting point. The official instructions presented to the King James translators as they began their work stipulated that the Bishops' Bible, the authorized Bible for use in the Church of England, was to be the English translation that was to be revised. But the fourteenth directive named five additional English Bibles, along with the statement that these should be "used when they agree better with the Text than the Bishops' Bible." It is obvious, then, that the King James Bible is a revision; in modern times such a version would stand a good chance of having the word *revised* or *new* in the title.

The sources that the translators consulted went far beyond just the English translations that had preceded the KJV. Translators went back to the original Hebrew and Greek texts. They consulted other translations than the six named, including non-English ones like Luther's German Bible and the Latin Vulgate. They consulted commentaries. They used the Syriac New Testament and the Aramaic Targums.[12]

Publication of the King James Bible

When the new translation was released to the public in 1611, the book that people held in their hands was a large and handsome volume, printed in black gothic lettering (not the easier-to-read roman lettering of the Geneva Bible), and typed in double columns on each page. It ran to fifteen hundred pages and was more than three inches thick.

The title page bore this extended title (here in modernized spelling): "The Holy Bible, containing the Old Testament and the New: Newly Translated out of the original Tongues: and with the former Translations diligently compared and revised, by his Majesty's special Commandment. Appointed to be read in churches." The last sentence is important, because it placed the new translation into the genre of official church Bibles like the Great Bible and Bishops' Bible. On the other hand, there is no evidence that the King James Bible was ever officially authorized by either the bishops or the king. In another quirk, the King James Bible has been known in many circles through the centuries as the AV, meaning the Authorized Version.

One more thing deserves to be said about the "authorization" of the King James Bible. As Geddes MacGregor astutely notes, the fact that the KJV did not receive official authorization allows us to see even more clearly the actual authority that the KJV commanded. Lacking official authorization, the King James Bible "made its own way as a book whose excellence was admitted on all sides," an authority "far greater than could have been conferred upon it by any legal instrument or official decree." The

King James Bible "was authorized, not by an edict imposed upon the people, but by popular acclamation."[13]

The original King James Bible had extensive preliminary material (such as an almanac accompanied by suggested Bible readings in the mornings and evenings, and tables of readings for the liturgical "holy days"). Of these documents, only two became familiar to posterity. First, since the king had commissioned the project, he received a flattering "Epistle Dedicatory." In contrast to this eminently forgettable document, the lengthy "The Translators to the Reader" is a landmark in English Bible translation and at certain places a Christian classic. Authored by Miles Smith, this wide-ranging preface covers such topics as the circumstances by which the King James Bible came into existence, the translation principles on which it is based, a defense of translating the Bible into the vernacular, and comments about the Bible that rank as devotional writing (see the accompanying excerpts).

Reception History

After its release, the King James Bible was not an immediate sensation, but it was a success, all the more surprising when we consider the obstacles that it had to overcome. The printer found himself in almost immediate financial difficulty, and the early years of printing were bound up in litigation. The Puritans were unenthusiastic about the new translation. A contentious scholar named Hugh Broughton, who had not been named to the translation committee, claimed that the translation contained hundreds of mistranslated words and warned the translators that they would be judged for their misconduct at the last day.

Considering these obstacles, the King James Bible did very well. The existing best-selling Bible, the Genevan, went into six editions between 1611 and 1614, compared with seventeen editions of the King James Bible. If we expand the time frame from 1611 to 1644, we find fifteen editions of the Geneva Bible, and a whopping 182 editions of the KJV.[14] In effect, the KJV supplanted the Geneva Bible within fifty years of its publication—very good indeed.

Excerpts from "The Translators to the Reader"

- "Translation . . . openeth the window, to let in the light; . . . that putteth aside the curtain, that we may look into the most Holy place; that removeth the cover of the well, that we may come by the water."

- [When the Bible is translated into English,] God "removeth the scales from our eyes, . . . that we may understand his word, enlarging our hearts, yea correcting our affections, that we may love it above gold and silver, yea that we may love it to the end. Ye are brought unto fountains of living water."

- Blessing will come to us if we "hearken, when [God] setteth his Word before us, to read it. . . . [May] the Lord work a care and conscience in us to know him and serve him, that we may be acknowledged of him at the appearing of our Lord Jesus Christ, to whom with the Holy Ghost, be all praise and thanksgiving. Amen."

While it might be expected that the Puritans would have given the Geneva Bible a boost during the era of their ascendancy and power in England, they did not do so. The last Geneva Bible (the competitor to the KJV) was published in England in 1616 and on the Continent in 1644. Perhaps we can see an acknowledgment of the merit of the King James translation in the fact that it was eventually printed with the Geneva Bible notes (at least nine editions between 1642 and 1715).[15] It was partly the notes and critical apparatus of the Geneva Bible that had made it supreme among the Bible-reading public.

With the restoration of the monarchy in 1660, the triumph of the King James Bible was secured. The Geneva Bible was disparaged because of its Puritan connections, and the KJV was the only viable alternative. The verdict of the noted Victorian New Testament scholar B. F. Westcott is thus correct: "From the middle of the seventeenth century, the King's Bible has been the acknowledged Bible of the English-speaking nations throughout the world simply because it is the best."

The fifty years from 1660 to 1710 consolidated the supremacy of the King James Bible. In these years, no new English translation was attempted, and 237 editions of the KJV were printed. Starting in 1662, all Bible readings in the Book of Common Prayer were from the King James Bible except the readings from the Psalms (where Coverdale was retained).[16]

The record of success of the King James Bible from 1700 to 1950 is indisputable. Although the first Puritan settlers in New England were devotees of the Geneva Bible, the first Bibles printed in America (the work of printer Robert Aitken of Philadelphia) were the King James Bible. David Daniell speaks of "the solid, near-absolute dependence of this new adventurous nation on KJV."[17] When the British and Foreign Bible and American Bible Society were founded in the early nineteenth century, they distributed astounding quantities of the KJV.[18]

Summary

The idea for the King James Bible was hatched at a low moment for evangelical Christianity at the Hampton Court Conference of 1604. Yet almost immediately the project elicited the best from a host of people—preeminently the translators themselves. The King James Bible entered the public sphere with a respectable showing, though at the time no one could have predicted that this Bible would become the book of books among English-speaking societies for nearly three centuries.

Further Reading

Gustavus S. Paine, *The Men Behind the King James Version* (1959).
Olga S. Opfell, *The King James Bible Translators* (1982).
Adam Nicolson, *God's Secretaries: The Making of the King James Bible* (2003).

4

THE KING JAMES BIBLE OF 1611

The King James Version . . . is greatly cherished. For genera-
tions, Christians and lovers of fine English have read the Bible
in this version. They have felt that its words spoke to them in a
particular way, in public or in private. . . . The very essence of
what Christians believe has been for centuries in the words of
that version.

—DAVID DANIELL, *The Bible in English*

THE PRECEDING CHAPTER HAS GIVEN ACCOUNT of how
the King James Bible came into existence and what happened
after it appeared. But what about the actual Bible that was first
published in 1611? This chapter is designed to answer that question. The focus will be on the King James Version as an English
translation. Chapter 8 will fill out the picture by examining the
King James Bible as a work of literature.

A Synthesis of Earlier Translations

The first thing that we can say about the King James Bible is
that it is an amalgamation of the English translations that had
preceded it in the sixteenth century. The tradition started with

Tyndale and then proceeded through Coverdale's Bible, Matthew's Bible, the Great Bible, the Geneva Bible, and the Bishops' Bible. The King James translators began with the Bishops' Bible as their starting point, but the Bishops' Bible itself was a conflation of the preceding century of English Bible translation.

"Fact Sheet" on the 1611 King James Bible

- The translators were experts in Hebrew and Greek, and in producing the KJV they consulted the original texts of the Bible, but they did not start from scratch. Technically the King James Bible is a revision of the Bishops' Bible. The case can be made that it is a revision of the entire preceding century of translation, starting with William Tyndale.

- Since the aim of the translation was to conserve what was best in the tradition of English Bible translation, the vocabulary of the King James Bible was just a trifle archaic already when it was published.

- Over 90 percent of the language of the King James Bible (including multiple occurrences of the same word) is native English rather than Latin-derived.

- The vocabulary of the King James Bible is approximately six to seven thousand words, compared with thirteen thousand for Milton and over twenty thousand for Shakespeare.

- By modern standards, the KJV is too heavily punctuated; the explanation is that the King James translators had in mind the oral reading and hearing of their translation, so they used punctuation to guide oral reading.

- Although the printer italicized words that had been added to what was in the original text, a comparison of the original version with later editions reveals that the original KJV was much more lightly italicized than later editions. The first round of italicizing was apparently inadequate to show the extent of what had been added to the original.

- The KJV was a forerunner of the modern practice of including scholarly notes on specific words to indicate either the literal meaning of a word or a legitimate alternate way of translating a word.

The King James translators themselves made no attempt to conceal their indebtedness to the past tradition. On the contrary, they highlighted their oneness with their predecessors. In the preface to the 1611 edition of the KJV, we read that the translators, "far from condemning any of their labors that travailed before us in this kind, . . . acknowledge them to have been raised up of God, for the building and furnishing of his Church, and that they deserve to be had of us and of posterity in everlasting remembrance."

We should not overlook the significance of that statement. First of all, there is an exemplary humility in the translators' attitude. Second, there is an impulse to give credit where credit is due, even though the King James translators obviously disagreed with their predecessors in many details. Third, as I will explore in the next chapter, there is an important principle of Bible translation at stake here, namely, continuity with the mainstream of English Bible translation versus the quest for originality and novelty (a deliberate attempt not to be like previous English translations). It is a fact that producers of modern dynamic equivalent translations often make disparaging comments about the King James Bible. One might wish for more of the graciousness of the King James translators, as well as their awareness that the grand tradition of English Bible translation is worthy to be perpetuated in many details.

Unfortunately, the almost automatic effect of seeing the facts and figures regarding the indebtedness of the King James Bible to its predecessors is to diminish the accomplishment of the KJV. We need steadfastly to resist this tendency. The King James Bible of 1611 consists of whatever is present in it, and it does not cease to exist simply because it was also in an earlier translation.

A Refinement of the Received Tradition

Another thing that often gets lost when we consider the indebtedness of the King James Bible to its predecessors is that the King James Bible is a refinement of the earlier translations and not simply an amalgamation of them. The translators themselves were as aware of this as they were aware of their assimilation of earlier translations, and the preface to the KJV attempts to make sure that readers will be aware of it. Here are two statements from the preface:

- "Yet for all that, as nothing is begun and perfected at the same time, and the later thoughts are thought to be the wiser: so if we building upon their foundation that went before us, and being helped by their labors, do endeavor to make that better which they left so good."
- "Whatsoever is sound already . . . the same will shine as gold more brightly, being rubbed and polished; also, if anything be halting, or superfluous, or not so agreeable to the original, the same may be corrected, and the truth set in place."

In view of the smoothness of flow for which the King James Bible is matchless, the statement in the preface about what is "halting" in earlier translations is particularly noteworthy. It shows that the translators were consciously seeking rhythmic excellence. Adam Nicolson notes that "Tyndale was working alone, in extraordinary isolation. His only audience was himself. And surely as a result there is a slightly bumpy, stripped straightforwardness about his matter and his rhythm." Even though Tyndale and the King James translators might agree in basic content, the King James translators "are memorable where Tyndale stumbles over his grammar."[1]

Although modern debunkers sometimes try to portray the King James translators as introducing inferior changes, the scholarly consensus has been that on balance the King James Bible is a refinement of what had preceded. This is not to deny that we can find passages in the King James Bible that are entries in the "what were they thinking?" category, such as this: "Through desire a man, having separated himself, seeketh *and* intermedleth with all wisdom" (Prov. 18:1). Nonetheless, it is indisputable

Refining a Text

Sixteenth-century translators could not have seen the process of refinement that was going on with the same clarity that we can see it with the advantage of temporal distance from the event. The process of change for the better that is evident in the following specimens was repeated hundreds of times. Here are three successive versions of John 15:12–13, reprinted in original spelling:

- Tyndale: "Thys ys my commaundement, that ye love togedder as I have loved you. Gretter love then this hath no man, then that a man bestowed his lyfe for his frendes."
- Geneva: "This is my commandement, that ye loue one another, as I haue loued you. Greater loue then this hathe no man, when any man bestoweth his life for his friends."
- KJV: "This is my Commaundement, that ye loue one another, as I have loued you. Greater loue hath no man then this, that a man lay downe his life for his friends."

Here are successive versions of Matthew 6:34b.

- Tyndale: "For the daye present hath ever ynough of his awne trouble."
- Coverdale: "Every daye hath ynough of his owne travayll."
- Great Bible: "Sufficient unto the daye is the travayle therof."
- Geneva: "The day hathe ynough with his owne grief."
- King James: "Sufficient unto the day is the evil thereof."

that the King James translators had wonderful intuitions in regard to retaining what was excellent and adding touches of improvement where they could. Here are representative scholarly statements:

- "Some of their adjustments had the Midas touch. . . . In a cumulative way, all the virtues of the various translations which preceded it were gathered up."[2]
- The KJV "was no sudden miracle but rather the harvesting or refining of the previous century's experience of translating the Bible into English."[3]

- "It forms a mosaic of all that was best in the work of preceding translators. . . . [Sometimes] the improvement is effected by a change in a word or two; but, in addition, there are entire clauses and sentences, the independent work of the Authorised Revisers, which have passed unscathed the critical tests of modern scholarship."[4]

- Conclusion drawn from a comparison of parallel passages in Tyndale, Geneva, and King James translations: "Even a superficial examination of the three renderings bears witness to the good judgment and taste of the revisers in selecting the best elements of preceding versions, and then adding a few fine touches of their own. . . . Omission of what is unnecessary to the thought is one of the effective means of heightening the style."[5]

- "Compared with its predecessors, the King James version shows a superb faculty of selection and combination, a sure instinct for betterment."[6]

A Translation Suited for Public Use

Another differentiating trait of the King James Bible is that it is preeminently a translation for public use. Of course its primary use through the centuries has been private reading. But that is true of all English Bible translations. The King James Bible shows its versatility by being ideally suited for oral use in public settings.

One of these public settings is worship in church services. In the centuries when the King James Bible was the standard Bible of Christendom, people in the pew heard something authoritative and beautiful when passages were read in the liturgical parts of a worship service, when the Lord's Prayer was prayed, when the passage for the sermon was read, and when verses from that passage reappeared during the course of the sermon. Twentieth-century Bible translator Edgar Goodspeed said that the KJV "occupies a place . . . in Christian liturgy that is . . . unique."[7]

But the public nature of the King James Bible was not limited to the church. As a later chapter will demonstrate, the degree to which the KJV lent itself to quotation in public discourse through the centuries has been breathtaking. Whenever a speaker, a politician, or a lawyer wanted to reference the Bible, the King James Bible was the translation of choice. And whenever the speaker quoted from the KJV, the effect was oracular. If we ask what makes the King James Bible so ideally suited for public use, the answer is twofold. First, it is an oral Bible, meaning that its rhythm flows smoothly off the tongue and into the ear of the listener. The second is a quality of the KJV that regularly gets registered by such words as *dignity* and *eloquence*. In later chapters I will explore the qualities of the KJV that elicit these impressions, but for the moment it is enough to note that the King James Bible has struck readers as possessing these qualities.

An Essentially Literal Translation

We get to the heart of the 1611 King James Bible when we consider how the translators lined up on the question of literal versus free translation. Of course the translators had no clue as to what would happen three and a half centuries after them with the advent of dynamic equivalent translation. It is all the more significant, therefore, that when left to their own designs the translators evolved the principle of verbal equivalence—the practice of making sure that every word in the original biblical text would be represented by an equivalent English word or phrase.

It is true that we need to infer this from the actual translation. The translators do not spell out their "essentially literal" philosophy, but neither do the prefaces of any other translation (even the RSV of 1952) until the NIV established the new philosophy of translation as the norm. Here is what Alister McGrath believes the King James translators aimed to do:[8]

1. Ensure that every word in the original was rendered by an English equivalent;
2. Make it clear when they added any words to make the sense clearer, or to lead to better English syntax. . . .
3. Follow the basic word order of the original wherever possible.

McGrath concludes that "the King James translators seem to have taken the view—which corresponds with the consensus of the day—that an accurate translation is, by and large, a literal and formal translation."[9]

An Accurate Translation

There can be little doubt that when the King James Bible was released in 1611, it was the most accurate English translation in existence. It was the product of the combined expertise of the four dozen best biblical scholars of their day, something that cannot be said of any previous English translation. The printed resources that these translators had at their disposal, though rudimentary by today's sophisticated standards, was the best available at the end of the sixteenth century. Donald Brake writes that "the new version won over its readers by sheer merit. Its faithfulness to the original languages and its fluid expressions as literature guaranteed its success."[10] C. B. McAfee is of the same opinion: "A second trait of the work as a version is its remarkable accuracy."[11]

Two things make it hard to get a fair hearing for the accuracy of the King James Bible today. One is the fact that the archaic language of the KJV is so acute for people unfamiliar with it that it is easy to conclude that it cannot be an accurate rendering of the original biblical text. The second is that the King James New Testament is based on original manuscripts that are today considered inferior. Both of these require brief exploration.

We can discern three levels of archaism in the King James Bible, as follows:

1. "One generation passeth away, and *another* generation cometh: but the earth abideth for ever" (Eccles. 1:4).
2. "For all his days *are* sorrows, and his travail grief" (Eccles. 2:23).
3. "I communed with mine own heart, saying, Lo, I am come to great estate" (Eccles. 1:16).

The first passage is archaic by virtue of its inflected verbs (*passeth*, *cometh*, *abideth*); it strikes us as an abnormal way of speaking, but the meaning is clear for anyone who makes an honest attempt to get beyond the inflected verbs. The word *travail* in the second example is not in most people's active vocabulary today, but it is in most Bible readers' passive vocabulary, or at least is a word that can be accurately construed from its context.

The archaisms in the third passage are more extreme. The formulations *communed with* and *great estate* use words whose meanings have changed during the past four centuries. Looking them up in the dictionary will not yield the meanings that the King James Bible has in view. If the words are not accurate by a modern lexicon, the translation needs to be judged inaccurate for a reader today. This is not to deny that a modern reader can be educated into what the words meant for the translators and their contemporary audience.

The overwhelming percentage of archaisms in the King James Bible fall into the first two categories. I find myself looking far and wide to find examples in the King James Bible of words whose meanings have changed so drastically that the translation can be called inaccurate. Perhaps the number of these passages is statistically insignificant. But for readers unfamiliar with the King James Bible, the mere presence of archaic language and constructions is usually interpreted as evidence that the King James Bible is inaccurate. This is a false impression.

The second strike that the KJV has against it in some circles is that the Greek text from which the translators worked is today not considered the most reliable. The King James translators (and all their sixteenth-century predecessors) used what is familiarly known as the Received Text (Textus Receptus). Older manuscripts than this have surfaced since the sixteenth century and are the basis of most modern translations of the New Testament.

We need to tread cautiously here: to say that the King James New Testament is based on manuscripts that are today con-sidered less than the best can superficially sound more sinister than in fact it is. If the Received Text is considered by most (not all) modern scholars as second-best, that does not mean that it is bad. The Greek text from which modern translators work is itself constantly being revised, so that a translation fifty years old might also be said to be based on less-than-the-best manuscripts. Additionally, the actual differences between the Received Text and modern conflated texts ("the Majority Text") are minor, and modern editions of the King James Bible indicate textual variants in scholarly footnotes, so no one is in danger of being misled by a modern edition of the KJV.[12]

Is the King James Bible Accurate Today?

The question of the accuracy of the King James Bible today is usually answered by looking only at the data that I considered in the preceding section. But quite another verdict surfaces when we place the King James Bible into the context of modern dynamic equivalent translations. Then suddenly the King James Bible zooms up on the scale of accuracy.

The reason for this is that the King James Bible is an essentially literal translation that aims to take the reader straight to what the original authors said. It is transparent to the original text. Here is a random example of the accuracy of the King James Bible as contrasted to modern dynamic equivalent translations (James 1:18b):

- ". . . that we should be a kind of firstfruits of his creatures" (KJV).
- "He wanted us to be his own special people" (CEV).
- "And we, out of all creation, became his choice possession" (NLT).
- ". . . so that we should have first place among all his creatures" (GNB).

Which of these is the most accurate? Surprise of surprises—the KJV is the most accurate because the translators gave us the equivalent English word with *firstfruits*. The original text says nothing about "special people," "choice possession," or "first place." It compares God's people to one of the Old Testament Mosaic produce offerings ("firstfruits").

Modern colloquializing translators lament that Bible translations run the risk of being further and further removed from the everyday language of people. This of course needs to be taken seriously. But an even worse problem is possible: many modern translations have moved further and further from the biblical text.

Here is a second example of the accuracy of the King James Bible even today. I recently participated in a year-long scholarly seminar on the Psalms. At one meeting, Psalm 131 was the text on the day's agenda. The leader circulated the NASB version of the text, which concludes the opening verse this way:

> Nor do I involve myself in great matters,
> Or in things too difficult for me.

This makes the forbidden knowledge a matter of intellectual complexity. Some modern translations agree with this interpretation (NKJV: "too profound"; HCSB: "too difficult"). An Old Testament scholar in the group then offered the information that current scholarship inclines to agree with "how the old versions translated the term." This naturally led to an inquiry about how the King James Bible renders the passage. The answer: "things too high for me"—not an intellectual challenge but spiritual and divine knowledge that is known only by a transcendent God.

I will offer one more personal anecdote. I recently listened to a sermon based on a passage in Galatians 4 that included verse 15. The NIV from which the preacher was preaching renders it, "What has happened to all your joy?" This makes it appear that the Galatian Christians were deficient in their religious emotions. My ears perked up when the preacher wondered aloud "whether the King James Bible doesn't say it best," despite its archaic language. The KJV reads, "Where is the blessedness you spake of?" The Galatians were not deficient in religious emotions but had allowed their "works righteousness" to obscure the true foundation of their religious standing with God, namely, the blessedness that God conferred on them by faith in the work of Christ. An anecdote like this should serve as a caution against a facile dismissal of the possibility that the King James Bible might represent accuracy (even a superior accuracy) in our day.

Whether or not the King James is an accurate version depends partly on how we define accuracy. If we believe that the standard of accuracy is a translation's giving us the words of the original text in equivalent English words, then the KJV shows its superior accuracy over modern dynamic equivalent translations on virtually every page of the Bible (and probably multiple times on every page).

Summary

When the 1611 King James Bible was published, it was a book that summed up and refined the preceding tradition of English Bible translation, and that represented accuracy of translation as understood within a translation philosophy of essentially literal translation. How noteworthy was the achievement of the King James Bible in these areas? I will end this chapter with a medley of scholarly quotations:

- "It grew to be a national possession and . . . is in truth a national classic. No other book has so penetrated and permeated the hearts and speech of the English race."[13]
- "If everything else in our language should perish it would alone suffice to show the whole extent of its beauty and power."[14]
- "And that was their triumph: a polished collation, a refinement of a century's translating, a book that became both clear and rich."[15]
- "It was the genius of the King James Version that it made [the word of God] speak so directly to those who heard it that though men knew it was a translation . . . they could never really think of it as such, for never did

a translation speak with such directness and lifegiving power."[16]

- "In popular Christian culture, the King James translation is seen to possess a dignity and authority that modern translations somehow fail to convey. . . . The King James Bible retains its place as a literary and religious classic, by which all others continue to be judged."[17]
- "On a historical scale, the sheer longevity of this version is a phenomenon, without parallel. . . . 'King James' is still the bestselling book in the world. . . . In the story of the earth we live on, its influence cannot be calculated."[18]
- "The Authorized Version is a miracle and a landmark. . . . There is no corner of English life, no conversation ribald or reverent that it has not adorned."[19]

Further Reading

H. Wheeler Robinson, ed., *The Bible in Its Ancient and English Versions* (1940).

Alister McGrath, *In the Beginning: The Story of the King James Bible and How It Changed a Nation, a Language, and a Culture* (2001).

Adam Nicolson, *God's Secretaries: The Making of the King James Bible* (2003).

PART TWO

The King James Bible
in History

5

The Influence of the King James Bible on the History of Bible Translation

The English Standard Version (ESV) stands in the classic main-stream of English Bible translations over the past half-millennium. . . . Our goal has been to carry forward . . . the Tyndale–King James legacy.

—Preface to the English Standard Version of the Bible

THE PURPOSE OF THIS CHAPTER is to trace the influence of the King James Version on Bible translation for the past three centuries. The first thing we need to note is that the King James Bible itself remained the dominant English Bible during most of that era. The most important influence of the KJV on the history of Bible translation was thus its continued presence as the preferred Bible of English-speaking Christians around the world (and not just in England and America). Its mere presence represented an influence.

A second thing is easily overlooked: the towering stature of the KJV among Bible readers meant that it influenced the subsequent history of English Bible translation by excluding other possible or actual translations. Even after the KJV started to show its age, especially in regard to archaic language, attempts to replace it largely failed until the appearance of the NIV in the 1970s. This is seen most dramatically when the Revised Version's New Testament hit the streets of London in 1881. The streets around the publishing house were blocked from dawn to dusk with processions of wagons being loaded with Bibles for transport. Leading newspapers in the United States had the text telegraphed for serial printing, and the new translation sold three hundred thousand copies the first day it was available in New York City. But after the dust had settled, the KJV did not have its supremacy undermined at all.

Third, and again easy to overlook, the King James Bible persisted as an influence on Bible translators who rejected it. When a member of the NIV translation team wrote that a modern translation must "not be intimidated by the King James Version peering over its shoulder,"[1] in that very repudiation the KJV functioned as an influence: it was a father figure who needed to be slain. When Eugene Peterson puts down the King James Bible for "its smooth, majestic sonorities,"[2] at that very moment the King James Bible is exerting its influence—the influence of an adversary.

Mainly, though, when we speak of the influence of the King James Bible on the subsequent history of Bible translation, we mean that there is a lineage of translations that consciously adhere to the translation philosophy and stylistic preferences of the KJV. The rest of this chapter will trace that lineage.

The Translations That Make Up the King James Tradition

There are three modern translations that are indisputably in the procession of the King James Bible. They are the Revised Standard Version of 1952, the New King James Bible of 1983, and the English Standard Version of 2001. Additional modern translations sometimes claim to be in this tradition, but it is not my task to

> "Translations eventually require revision, not necessarily because they are defective, but because . . . language . . . changes over time. . . . The true heirs of the King James translators are those who continue their task today, not those who declare it to have been definitively concluded in 1611."
> —Alister McGrath, *In the Beginning*

enlarge the boundaries of my discussion to include doubtful candidates. *To the degree to which* additional translations incorporate the principles and style of the King James Bible, they too operate under the influence of the King James tradition.

I need to stay one more moment with this "gray area" that has emerged in recent years. The preface to the New American Standard Bible (NASB) makes no claim to be in the King James tradition, and this is as it should be, inasmuch as the NASB is a revision of the American Standard Version of 1901. Yet in its adherence to the principle of translating all of the actual words of the original Hebrew and Greek into equivalent English words, the NASB belongs to the King James tradition. On the other side, the New Revised Standard Version wants to align itself with the King James tradition, but its actual adherence to it is halfhearted.

The preceding chapter of this book has identified the leading features of the King James Bible, and a later chapter devoted to its literary qualities will fill out the picture. Because I will have thus demonstrated elsewhere how the principles underlying the King James Bible are present in the actual translation, I will assume that as a background for the modern translations that I discuss in this chapter. For my purposes in this chapter, instead of beginning with the King James Bible, I have derived my material from the prefaces to the three Bibles that make up the King James tradition in modern times. We can trust these prefaces to delineate the features of the KJV that have been perpetuated in the respective translations, and it turns out that these prefaces are largely in agreement in their definitions of what constitutes the King James tradition.

Continuity with the Mainstream of English Bible Translation

In earlier chapters of this book we saw the astonishing degree to which English Bible translators of the sixteenth century viewed their work as an unfolding story in which the successive English Bibles were chapters of a larger narrative. Individual translators and committees were totally uninterested in being original. Instead they retained as much as they could of their forerunners, making improvements and refinements in what was regarded as a shared body of material. The culminating statement of this philosophy was the statement of the King James translators that they "never thought from the beginning, that we should need to make a new translation, nor yet to make of a bad one a good one, . . . but . . . out of many good ones, one principal good one."

"The King James translators . . . stood in a long line of translators, and were conscious that their task would be influenced . . . by the English translations already in circulation. . . . Lying behind this is an attitude toward wisdom that has largely been lost in the modern period. . . . The King James Bible . . . is to be seen in the light of the Renaissance approach to human wisdom, in which one generation is nourished and sustained by the intellectual achievements of its predecessors. Each era draws on the wisdom of the past, and builds upon it, before handing a greater wisdom on to its successors." —Alister McGrath, *In the Beginning*

This attitude toward continuity with what is excellent in the history of Bible translation is highlighted in the prefaces to the three modern translations that represent the King James tradition in the modern era. The preface to the RSV was the first to sound the keynote. Early in the preface the translators cite the KJV itself as a model for assimilating rather than repudiating its predecessors: "The translators who made the King James Version took into account all of these preceding versions; and comparison shows that it owes something to each of them. It kept felicitous phrases and apt expressions, from whatever source, which had stood the test of public usage." The RSV translators then express their commitment to the same principle: "In the end the decision was reached [to] . . . stay as close to the Tyndale–King James tradition as it can in the light of our present knowledge of the Hebrew and Greek texts and their meaning on the one hand, and our present understanding of English on the other."

The preface to the New King James Version repeats these themes. It begins by recalling that the 1611 KJV was "indebted to the earlier work of William Tyndale and others," and additionally that the translators of the KJV "saw their best contribution to consist in revising and enhancing the excellence of the English versions which had sprung from the Reformation of the sixteenth century." Applying the same principle to their own work, the translators of the NKJV state, "In harmony with the purpose of the King James scholars, the translators and editors of the present work have not pursued a goal of innovation. They have perceived the Holy Bible, New King James Version, as a continuation of the labors of the earlier translators."

The preface to the ESV makes the same claims for continuity with the King James tradition. The ESV "stands in the classic mainstream of English Bible translations over the past half-millennium." "The words and phrases themselves," we are told, "grow out of the Tyndale–King James legacy."

The ramifications of this sense of continuity are far-reaching. Of course it means that the three translations I have cited adhere to the translation principles and style of the King James Bible (see below). But we need to pause and take stock before we move on to those points. When a translation committee places itself on the side of continuity, a certain safeguard immediately "kicks in." It is a fact that translations in the King James tradition generally avoid the idiosyncratic and produce stable renditions of the biblical text, subject of course to changes in vocabulary as the years unfold.

What about modern translations that do not embrace continuity with the King James tradition? To begin, we will consult the prefaces of those translations in vain to find any reference to fellowship with other translations. The translators of these

> "I have used the revised Standard Version (RSV) in this anthology because it is written in a contemporary style that still preserves almost all the phrases and cadences of the King James Version that have entered the English literary tradition." —David Curzon, *The Gospels in Our Image*

versions want to be original and innovative. Furthermore, as the dynamic equivalence movement unfolded, successive translations became more and more daring in departing from established norms in their rendering of the biblical text. The result is what I have elsewhere called destabilization of the biblical text. By this I mean that the non-KJV translations often show wide variance in their rendering of the same biblical passage.

Related to this is a difference in how the two sets of translators view themselves. Translation committees that want to be innovative and untied to other translations exhibit a lone-wolf mentality. I do not intend that in a wholly pejorative sense; these translators have no alternative but to be individualistic once they accept the premise that they wish *not* to be like the King James tradition. Still, these translators need to "own" the result of their outlook, which is a tendency to be singular in many of their renditions of the biblical text.

Essentially Literal Translation

No principle is more central to the King James tradition than the principle that today goes by the name of "essentially literal translation." This label denotes that the first task of Bible translators (whatever additional tasks might eventually come into play) is to find equivalent English words for all of the words (but not *more* than all of the words) that appear in the original Hebrew and Greek texts. This premise immediately rules out three practices that have become standard features of modern dynamic equivalent translations. Here are the practices that are *disallowed* by the "essentially literal" platform but that are the bread-and-butter methodology of dynamic equivalent translations:

- Omitting words found in the original text (for example, dropping metaphors and other figurative language)
- Substituting words or phrases for what is in the original text, usually accompanied by claims that the substitute formulations express the same meaning as the original words
- Adding commentary to what is found in the original text

Standing opposed to these procedures is essentially literal translation, based on the premise of verbal equivalence (making sure that every word in the original text has found an equivalent English word or phrase in the English translation). Again the prefaces and surrounding documents of modern translations in the King James tradition signal what the translators have done.

Even though the RSV appeared before the dynamic equivalent movement was fully evident, it was governed solidly by an essentially literal philosophy. Here is the manifesto stated by one of the translators: the translator "is charged to tell as accurately as he can in his own language precisely what the original says. . . . The Bible translator assumes a strict responsibility to say in English just what the Biblical writers said in Hebrew, or in Aramaic or in Greek. . . . The Bible translator is not an expositor."[3]

By the time the NKJV appeared (1983), dynamic equivalence had swept the field of English Bible translation. The preface to it accordingly throws down the gauntlet to the dynamic equivalence movement. The banner under which the translators chose to sail is "complete equivalence in translation." By this they meant that their translation sought "to preserve *all* of the information in the text."

As required by the new context in which translation was now occurring, the translators further contrasted their methodology to that of dynamic equivalence: "Dynamic equivalence, a recent procedure in Bible translation, commonly results in paraphrasing where a more literal rendering is needed." The formula *complete equivalence* was a happy invention, but the

NKJV preface does not fully articulate the principle of verbal equivalence (preserving the very words of the original text in equivalent English words). Nonetheless the composers of the preface mention a very helpful pair of concepts when they praise the King James Bible for its "precision of translation" (i.e., its accuracy in rendering the words of the original) as well as its "majesty of style."

Continuity and Discontinuity with the King James Tradition (Ps. 34:19)

- KJV: "Many *are* the afflictions of the righteous: but the LORD delivereth him out of them all."
- RSV: "Many are the afflictions of the righteous; / but the LORD delivers him out of them all."
- NKJV: "Many *are* the afflictions of the righteous, / But the LORD delivers him out of them all."
- ESV: "Many are the afflictions of the righteous, / but the LORD delivers him out of them all."
- NIV: "A righteous man may have many troubles, / but the LORD delivers him from them all."
- NLT: "The righteous face many troubles, / but the LORD rescues them from each and every one."
- MESSAGE: "Disciples so often get into trouble; / still, GOD is there every time."

It was left to the ESV preface to complete the unfolding evolution of essentially literal translation. The preface comes right out and identifies its procedure as "word-for-word correspondence" between the original and English texts at a verbal level, but not necessarily at the levels of grammar, syntax, and idiom. A new level of sophistication also enters with the concept that the goal of such verbal equivalence is "to be transparent to the original text, letting the reader see as directly as possible the structure and meaning of the original." Not surprisingly, this preface, too, presents its essentially literal philosophy as an alternative to dynamic equivalence.

The King James translators were so scrupulous about *words* that they italicized words in their translation that were needed for the English sense but that were not present in the original text. The goal was obviously to avoid confusing the reader and contrariwise to keep the reader fully informed. I cannot avoid contrasting that procedure to dynamic equivalent translations, where the effect is to keep readers clueless as to what the original says and uninformed regarding where the words of Scripture end and the commentary of the translators begins.

What is the result of verbal equivalence as a translation philosophy? To answer that question, all we need to do is read the three translations that are my focus. They are essentially literal, preserving the words of the original in equivalent English words. For a more thorough proof of this, I invite my readers to read my two books on English Bible translation.[4]

The Style of the King James Bible

The third theme that uniformly surfaces in the prefaces of modern translations that align themselves with the King James tradition concerns style. I propose first to look at the statements from the prefaces themselves and then extract the essence of the King James style as perceived by modern translators.

Because the RSV appeared before the rival movement known as dynamic equivalence had surfaced, its preface again has the least to say because there was no perceived threat to the translators' position. The preface has the following brief comment: "We have resisted the temptation to use phrases that are merely current usage, and have sought to put the message of the Bible in simple, enduring words that are worthy to stand in the great Tyndale–King James tradition."

The preface to the New King James Version spells the matter out in slightly more detail. The first descriptor is the phrase "majesty of style." Later the preface quotes with approval a Catholic scholar who had praised the KJV for how it had "achieved a beautifully artistic result." Third, the preface endorses "that lyrical quality which is so highly regarded in the Authorized Version."

On the production of the RSV: "There was inevitably a difference between those who wanted a textually conservative revision and those who . . . desired a radical departure from the tradition of English Bible revision and the production of a more colloquial version. Moffatt represented a moderate position on this question, seeking to modernize the English thoroughly, yet always bearing in mind the principle that the Committee's task was to continue the revision of the King James Version, not to supplant it with a radically new translation. He helped much to guide the Committee toward the production of a version whose language, though brought up to date in all respects, would nevertheless conserve the dignity of the beloved King James Version, not unnecessarily offending the ears of those who were accustomed to the use of this [dignity] in public worship." —Geddes MacGregor, *A Literary History of the Bible*

The preface also hints at the stylistic range and flexibility of the KJV when it notes a "devotional quality" in the prophetic and poetic books, and "plain style of the gospels and epistles." Finally, almost as an afterthought, the preface uses the formula "majestic and reverent style."

The preface to the ESV states that the translation "carries forward classic translation principles in its literary style." This is spelled out in terms of the retention of theological vocabulary, preservation of the stylistic variety of the original text, maintaining the flow of sentences as the original text expresses itself, and decisions regarding gender language.

In regard to following the style of the King James Bible, the three prefaces tell us less than the actual translations do. The composers of the prefaces want to align themselves with something that they cherish in the style of the KJV, but they understate the case that can be made for the congruence of their translations with the stylistic excellence of the KJV. Showing the ways in which these translations measure up admirably to the King James standard, though in modern vocabulary and syntax, is beyond the scope of this book (though again I commend my detailed treatment of the topic in my earlier books on modern translations).

In brief, the stylistic traits that modern translations in the King James tradition perpetuate are these:

- exaltation and affective power
- dignity of vocabulary and avoidance of a colloquial style
- relatively sophisticated phraseology and syntax
- smoothness of rhythm
- retention of figurative language
- refusal to turn the concrete vocabulary of the original into abstractions

Summary

Modern translations exist on a continuum with a "great divide" in the middle in regard to continuity with the King James tradition versus departure from it. Some translators want to be placed in the tradition; others distance themselves from it by silence, though if one reads beyond the prefaces to statements by the translators, a genuine hostility to the King James tradition often emerges. When modern translations position themselves in the King James tradition, they identify their allegiance in terms of fidelity to reproduce in English the words of the original and a style that they aspire to uphold.

Further Reading

Raymond C. Van Leeuwen, "We Really Do Need Another Bible Translation," *Christianity Today*, October 22, 2001, 28–35.
Leland Ryken, *The Word of God in English* (2002).
Leland Ryken, *Understanding English Bible Translation* (2009).

6

THE INFLUENCE OF THE KING JAMES BIBLE ON LANGUAGE, EDUCATION, AND RELIGION

No other book of any kind ever written in English, perhaps no other book ever written in any other tongue, has ever so affected the whole life of a people as this authorized version of the Scriptures has affected the life of the English-speaking peoples.

—THEODORE ROOSEVELT, *Realizable Ideals*

I WANT TO START AT THE BROADEST possible level by defining the concept of cultural "mythology." A sociologist has provided the following definition, and I will note in passing that I use this as a framework for the literature courses that I teach and sometimes for the literary criticism that I publish: "The mythology of a culture is the framework of beliefs, values, expressive symbols, and artistic motifs in terms of which individuals define their world, express their feelings, and make their judgments."[1]

For nearly four centuries, the King James Bible provided such a framework for England and America.

George Lindbeck, a former professor of theology at Yale University, has described this with helpful clarity. Until recently, writes Lindbeck, "most people in traditionally Christian countries lived in the linguistic and imaginative world of the Bible."[2] "The text above all texts," Lindbeck continues, "was the [King James] Bible. Its stories, images, conceptual patterns, and turns of phrase permeated the culture from top to bottom." Nor did this influence depend solely on personal reading of the Bible, but it was instead "true even for illiterates and those who did not go to church, for knowledge of the Bible was transmitted not only directly by its reading, hearing, and ritual enactment, but also indirectly by an interwoven net of intellectual, literary, artistic, folkloric, and proverbial traditions." The "bottom line" is that "Christendom dwelt imaginatively in the biblical world."

The division of duties between this chapter and the next is a little arbitrary. The current chapter covers topics that relate broadly to individual, family, and religious spheres. The ensuing chapter will explore the general cultural influence of the King James Version.

The King James Bible and the English Language

That the King James Bible has been the largest single influence on the English language is often asserted and can be plausibly inferred, but it is of course hard to prove. The witness of experts counts for something:

- "The King James Bible, along with the works of William Shakespeare, is regularly singled out as one of the most foundational influences on the development of the modern English language. . . . 'Biblical English' came to possess a cultural authority on the same level as that of Shakespeare."[3]
- "No other text in the history of the English language has done as much as the [King James] Bible to shape

our modern idiom. . . . What the Bible did was bring standard English . . . into the forefront of people's attention. . . . The general style of the English language has been so influenced by the Bible because of this public presence."[4]

- "The [AV] English Bible has to a marvelous extent shaped our speech, giving peculiar connotations to many words, and sanctioning strange constructions."[5]

The most customary way by which to demonstrate the influence of the King James Bible on the English language is to list the familiar idioms and proverbs that English-speaking people have owed to the KJV through the centuries. Any list of these sayings and expressions is necessarily selective; the following list will serve as well as any other.

- "The land of the living" (Job 28:13).
- "I will wash my hands in innocency" (Ps. 26:6).
- "At their wit's end" (Ps. 107:27).
- "Heap coals of fire on his head" (Prov. 25:22; Rom. 12:20).
- "There is no new thing under the sun" (Eccles. 1:9).
- "The salt of the earth" (Matt. 5:13).
- "A prophet is not without honour save in his own country" (Matt. 13:57).
- "The signs of the times" (Matt. 16:3).
- "In the twinkling of an eye" (1 Cor. 15:52).
- "The root of the matter" (Job 19:28).
- "Fire and brimstone" (Ps. 11:6).
- "A law unto themselves" (Rom. 2:14).
- "Labour of love" (1 Thess. 1:3).
- "Old wives' fables" (1 Tim. 4:7).
- "As a lamb to the slaughter" (Isa. 53:7).
- "Fell flat on his face" (Num. 22:31).
- "Filthy lucre" (1 Tim. 3:3).

> "But beyond even its poetry, I was impressed by it as a treasury of *gnomic* [proverbial] wisdom. I mean its richness in utterances of which one could, as it were, chew the cud. This, of course, has long been recognized, and Biblical sentences have passed into the proverbial wisdom of our country."
> —Victorian poet Francis Thompson, "Books That Have Influenced Me"

The Bible quotations that appear in *Bartlett's Familiar Quotations* have been segregated out and published as a freestanding book entitled *Bartlett's Bible Quotations*.[6] The book is over two hundred pages long. The editor explains in the preface that "all quotations come from the Authorized Version of the Bible, . . . surely the most influential book ever published in the English language." The editor also correctly states that the famous quotations "were introduced by the King James Bible, [were] picked up in English vernacular, and entered popular imagination."

What does a book like *Bartlett's Bible Quotations* show? Quite a lot. It shows first that the King James Bible possesses the linguistic and stylistic qualities that enabled it to become the major influence on the development of the English language. To take an example, the phrase "labour of love" is inherently aphoristic, whereas the following renditions would never have stuck in the memory even if the respective translations had enjoyed the cultural dominance of the KJV: "labor prompted by love" (NIV), "loving deeds" (NLT), "loving work" (CEV). Second, the familiarity of sayings like the ones listed demonstrates again how pervasive the KJV became in the English-speaking world.

The KJV as an Influence on Non-Western Cultures

The influence of the King James Bible on the English language is a good entry point for an excursion into a little-recognized subject, namely, the King James Bible as a non-Western influence. Over my years of teaching at a Christian college I have observed a steady flow of students from such regions as Africa, India, China, and Hong Kong who received English-speaking educations in their native countries. Usually the schools that they attended were established by missionaries and not (as we commonly think) as British colonial enterprises. The chief lesson that I have learned from this flow of students is that until recently the phenomenon of "the English Bible" automatically meant the KJV.

Published sources yield preliminary and limited evidence of what is well known to be a fact, and I will start with them. David Daniell briefly tells the story of the influence of the English and American Bible societies.[7] He entitles the unit covering this material "KJV for the World," and in noting some of the statistics on print runs he comments parenthetically, "all, of course, KJV." In the same vein, Alister McGrath writes that "the triumph of the King James Bible was not limited to Great Britain. . . . The expansion of British economic and military influence in the later eighteenth and nineteenth centuries was preceded and accompanied by missionary work, based on the King James Bible."[8] And Benson Bobrick writes that "Englishmen carried their Bible with them . . . overseas, even as it came to live in their own language with more abiding force. . . . Its impact on thought and culture eventually spread the world over, 'as wide as the waters be.'"[9]

A similar story is told by people who recall receiving an English education in non-Western countries. The author of a book on the Bible in Africa records that "where education had to be given in the colonial language, the French Bible translation of Louis Segond or the classical King James Bible was used."[10] The foremost contemporary authority on the Bible in the third world speaks of the KJV as "an undisputed universal script" and "the most venerated icon of British culture," noting additionally that the King James Bible was for "two centuries . . . triumphantly hailed as the book of the Empire."[11]

"'King James' is still the bestselling book in the world. Geographically, its spread has been global for hundreds of years: wherever in the world there are English readers, there are copies." —David Daniell, *The Bible in English*

The main evidence for the influence of the King James Bible beyond England and America comes from the statements of people who experienced that influence in their own lives. Marie Friesema of the English department at Wheaton College grew up as a Filipino in the Philippines.[12] Her education and church life were conducted in English. For her, the KJV was the sole translation used right through the 1970s. Sermons used the KJV, and Bible memory was from the KJV, a pattern common to evangelical churches in the Philippines. Additionally, the King James Bible was a key ingredient in language acquisition, and Marie testifies that "the King James Version of the Bible has been the best English language teacher I ever had."

A similar story emerges from the English-speaking subculture of India. Vijai John of Wheaton, Illinois, grew up as a Catholic in southern India. He recalls that the English Bibles that were available free through such organizations as the Gideons and the Bible Society of India were King James Bibles.[13] It was such a Bible that Vijai himself received as a first-grader, and he used the KJV during his college years in an Anglican college. The "Bible churches" in Vijai's region of India had a strong preference for the KJV and sometimes regarded other English translations as spurious. Language acquisition is a theme here, too, as parents encouraged their children to read from the KJV rather than other English translations to gain an appreciation for the beauty of its language.

Dr. Sam Hsu, professor of music at Philadelphia Biblical University, was born in Shanghai, China, in the middle of the twentieth century. While Sam's brother received his orientation to the King James translation as part of the British system of general education at an Anglican school, Sam's exposure to the KJV came by way of American missionaries in Hong Kong.[14] Instruction in the Bible and memorization from it centered in the King James translation. Dr. Hsu claims that the "KJV remains the pattern of intuition as I recall passages of Scripture."

Dr. Johann Buis, professor of music at Wheaton College, spent his early life as a native South Africaner. According to Buis, the King James Bible arrived in South Africa with the London Missionary Society in 1799.[15] The KJV remained "authoritative" in black communities until the 1970s, and even after that some conservative evangelical churches clung to the KJV. Buis notes further that part of the cultural influence of the King James Bible is that its formal and poetic language became a "special" language used in formal discourse, especially addresses to deity and monarchy.

We can catch one more glimpse into the King James Bible as an influence in the English-speaking subcultures of non-Western countries in Nigerian author Chinua Achebe. In an autobiographical essay entitled "The Education of a British-Protected Child," Achebe speaks of "daily portions of the Bible we read at prayer time every morning and every night."[16] But which English Bible? Scattered quotations in Achebe's fiction quote the KJV almost verbatim: "Why do the nations rage and the people imagine a vain thing? He that sitteth in the heavens shall laugh. The Lord shall have them in derision" (*Things Fall Apart*). "The people which sat in darkness saw a great light and to them which sat in the region and shadow of death, to them did the light spring up" (*No Longer at Ease*, where the passage is printed as poetry).

No English Bible became the dominant influence in third-world countries to the extent that the KJV became the primary framework in England and America. But the KJV held a lofty place in English-speaking subcultures within those countries. The anecdotal evidence that I have adduced gives us snapshots of that influence, and I have devoted attention to it in order to counter a common misconception that Britain and North America are the only countries where the King James Bible exerted a cultural influence.

The Devotional and Church Lives of Christians

The most important sphere in which the King James Bible permeated English and American culture for approximately four centuries is the daily and weekly religious lives of Christians. My own experience illustrates the pattern that prevailed in some form in millions of families over the centuries. I heard the King James Bible read after meals three times every day. I heard it read and preached on from the pulpit twice every Sunday. A passage from the KJV was printed conspicuously in the Sunday school handout on Sunday mornings. Bible memorization was based on the KJV both at church and at Christian schools. When a representative from the Gideons handed out maroon-colored New Testaments at my school, the translation was the KJV. When I was nine my parents gave me a King James Bible as a Christmas gift, and I used it right through my college years.

In bygone eras, Christians customarily hung plaques displaying Bible verses on the walls in their homes (a practice whose decline seems to have coincided with the rise of alternate modern translations). When I left home for graduate school, newly married, I confiscated a plaque from my parental home that bore the verse that my pastor had earmarked for me when I made public profession of faith. The verse was reproduced from the King James Bible: "I can do all things through Christ, which strengtheneth me" (Phil. 4:13). Hanging in a room in my house to this day is the plaque that I made from the letters of dry alphabet soup in the third grade: "Blessed is he whose transgression is forgiven, whose sin is covered" (Ps. 32:1).

The scenario I have described prevailed in evangelical and even "high-church" circles from the mid-seventeenth century through the 1960s. In the Victorian era, for example, the high-church Anglican Christina Rossetti and the heterodox Anglican Florence Nightingale were continuous readers of the Bible, not only personally but in household devotions.[17] To make the Bible central to religious life meant to elevate the King James Bible; there was no rival English Bible.

In England, the exposure to the King James Bible in a church setting was intensified by the centrality of the Prayer Book in church services. For over two centuries (starting in 1662) the readings from the Psalms were printed in Coverdale's translation, but all other readings were from the KJV. This means that all readings from the Epistles and Gospels on Sunday mornings were from the King James Bible. A person attending a Christmas church service in Victorian England would hear the following at the outset of the reading from the Epistle: "God, who at sundry times and in divers manners spake in time past unto the fathers by the prophets, hath in these last days spoken unto us by his Son." Additionally, it seems likely that to the person in the pew the dignity and exaltation of the prayers would have seemed cut from the same cloth as the King James passages, even though they are not a direct quotation from a single passage: "Almighty God, who hast given us thy only-begotten Son to take our nature upon him . . . , grant that we being regenerate and made thy children by adoption and grace, may daily be renewed by thy Holy Spirit; through the same our Lord Jesus Christ, who liveth and reigneth with thee . . . world without end" (Christmas Day collect).

Public inscriptions in religious places tell the same story of the KJV as the default Bible for English-speaking Christians. In the Presbyterian church in suburban St. Louis where I was married, a gold-gilt Bible verse has been posted on the wall behind the pulpit and platform for decades. It reads, "For God so loved the world, that he gave his only begotten Son, that whosoever believeth in him should not perish, but have everlasting life." As I look up from a pew at Tenth Presbyterian Church in Philadelphia, I can see the following verses on memorial plaques on the walls, all from the KJV: "he being dead yet speaketh" (Heb. 11:4); "being made conformable unto his death" (Phil. 3:10); "well done, thou good and faithful servant, thou hast been faithful over a few things, I will make thee ruler over many things; enter thou into the joy of thy Lord" (Matt. 25:21).

When I last visited the Lake District in northern England, I spent time inside St. Oswald Church in Grasmere. English poet William Wordsworth is buried in the churchyard. I immediately noticed twenty "admonitory texts on framed boards," as a booklet available for sale in the church calls them. The booklet explains that these wooden boards, "which were put up in 1711 and replaced similar texts painted on the plastered walls, . . . could be studied by those who could read, and whose eyesight was good enough." Two specimen texts are these: "Come unto me, all ye that labour and are heavy-laden, and I will give you rest"; "I know that my Redeemer liveth and that he shall stand at the latter day upon the earth." Even the recently printed booklet quotes from the KJV, as in the observation that the clear glass in the east window calls to mind the opening verse of Psalm 121: "I will lift up mine eyes unto the hills from whence cometh my help."

> "There was a time when every educated person, no matter how professedly unbelieving or secular, knew the actual text from Genesis to Revelation. . . . Once [dominant cultural texts] penetrate deeply into the psyche, especially the collective psyche, they cease to be primarily objects of study and rather come to supply the conceptual and imaginative vocabularies . . . with which to construe and construct reality." —George Lindbeck, "The Church's Mission to a Postmodern Culture"

No scientific survey exists to prove my assertions about how the King James Bible was the atmosphere within which Christians lived and moved and had their being for nearly four centuries. But we do not need such a survey. The random snapshots that I have provided prove what we all know and can verify simply by keeping our antennae up when we have contact with the religious cultures of the past and in some quarters of the present (inasmuch as the KJV is still the second-best-selling English Bible).

Education

The best starting point for exploring the impact of the KJV on education is childhood learning, especially early acquisition of literacy. One scholar claims that "it is from [the KJV] that the English-speaking world learned to read and to think."[18] Someone else has written that "the greatest vehicle of literacy in the English-speaking world has been the King James Bible. It has been the great primer."[19] What David Daniell says of the eighteenth century in England continued for two more centuries in both

Great Britain and America: "KJV's national grip remained in the family and school as well as in church."[20]

We can catch a glimpse of what this looked like in practice in a statement by Daniel Webster, whose devotion to the Bible and ability to quote it from memory were legendary. Here is Webster's recollection of his early contact with the Bible:

> From the time that at my mother's feet or on my father's knee I first learned to lisp verses from the sacred writings, they have been my daily study and vigilant contemplation. If there be anything in my style or thoughts to be commended, the credit is due to my kind parents in instilling into my mind an early love of the Scriptures.[21]

One scholar's comment on the passage is this: "These words . . . tell of a mighty educational factor, not only in the life of the man who uttered them, but also in the life of an entire English-speaking world."[22]

According to historian Christopher Hill, in the sixteenth and seventeenth centuries "boys and girls learnt to read from the Bible."[23] When this cultural trend began, the Bible that was used for education was usually the Geneva Bible, but as it was supplanted by the KJV, the latter was the Bible with which children learned to read. For example, during the teaching career of American educator William McGuffey "students brought their own books [to school], most frequently the Bible, since few textbooks existed."[24] But when textbooks *were* available, the King James Bible was prominent in the contents of those books.

The New England Primer, for example, has interspersed biblical sections, including "an alphabet of lessons for youth." It consists of alphabetically arranged verses from the King James Bible: "Except a man be born again, he cannot see the kingdom of God" (John 3:3); "Many are the afflictions of the righteous, but the LORD delivereth them out of them all" (Ps. 34:19). The most widely used schoolbook of the nineteenth century in America was *McGuffey's Eclectic Reader* series, and the interspersed biblical passages are straight from the KJV (e.g., Paul's defense before King

"It was standard practice for Victorian children to learn to read on the Authorized Version . . . of the Bible. The Bible was the primary text in schools. . . . [Before 1870] many poor children received all the formal education they would ever have from a church. . . . Even in independent, working-class schools the Bible was still the standard book." —Timothy T. Larsen, "Literacy and Bible Knowledge: The Victorian Age and Our Own"

"In [Victorian] working-class private school . . . the Bible and the Testament . . . were frequently used—especially in 'common day' schools—for learning to read or for reading practice." —Phil Gardner, *The Lost Elementary Schools of Victorian England: The People's Education*

Agrippa in the fifth reader and Psalm 104 in the sixth reader). A biographer of McGuffey and expert on the *Reader* series notes, "Since McGuffey felt that knowing the Bible was of utmost importance in a child's education, he included many lessons about the Bible, in addition to using much material from the Old and New Testaments."[25]

In an essay cited earlier in this chapter Yale University professor George Lindbeck stated, "When I first arrived at Yale, even those who came from nonreligious backgrounds knew the Bible better than most of those now who come from churchgoing families."[26] One reason for the familiarity in earlier eras is that until the middle of the twentieth century the King James Bible was part of public school education. In the one-room rural school that my father briefly attended as a boy, students were asked to respond to roll call by spontaneously quoting a Bible verse. (My father once unwittingly elicited laughter by choosing Proverbs 6:6: "Go to the ant, thou sluggard; consider her ways, and be wise.") The decline in biblical literacy among the churched that Lindbeck records coincided with the replacement of the KJV by modern translations.

We should not think of the KJV influence on education as a factor only in the remote past. Until 1970 the King James Bible remained the dominant English Bible in Christian circles, and it is still the preferred English Bible in some Christian schools.

Although the Bible gradually receded from view in public education during the twentieth century, it was always the central text in Christian education, whether in the family, the church, or Christian grade schools, high schools, and colleges.

Religious Discourse

Another huge sphere of King James Bible influence is religious discourse. This encompasses sermons preached in church, evangelistic sermons, and published works by Christian scholars and authors. From the mid-seventeenth century to the mid-twentieth century, we can picture virtually all of the famous Christian speakers and religious writers as using the King James Bible. A few random snapshots will suffice to illustrate that claim.

As I recently perused a booklet with excerpts from the past on the subject of justification, it was obvious that for several centuries the KJV was the common Bible of evangelical Protestantism. Here are the names of the theologians and preachers included in the booklet, accompanied by a specimen biblical quotation from each treatise that was excerpted:

- *Charles Spurgeon.* "Being justified freely by his grace through the redemption that is in Christ Jesus" (Rom. 3:24).
- *Charles Hodge.* "All the people that heard him, and the publicans, justified God" (Luke 7:29).
- *A. W. Pink.* "With the heart man believeth unto righteousness" (Rom. 10:10).
- *Horatius Bonar.* "Not by works of righteousness which we have done, but according to his mercy he saved us" (Titus 3:5).
- *J. C. Ryle.* "There is no peace, saith my God, to the wicked" (Isa. 57:21).

Just as we usually do not think to ask what specific English Bible the great English and American literary authors used, it is easy not to ask what English Bible the towering religious figures of the past used. What Bible did Jonathan Edwards use? Edwards's delightful *Personal Narrative* provides a ready answer. The scattered biblical quotations are from the KJV: "Now unto the King eternal, immortal, invisible, the only wise God, be honour and glory for ever and ever, Amen" (1 Tim. 1:17). "My soul breaketh for the longing it hath" (Ps. 119:20). "A man shall be an hiding place from the wind, and a covert from the tempest" (Isa. 32:2).

What about Charles Spurgeon, who preached to thousands upon thousands at the Metropolitan Tabernacle in London? A quick look into Spurgeon's sermons, commentaries on books of the Bible, or devotional books like *Morning and Evening* will answer the question at once: Spurgeon used the King James Bible. He also endorsed it as the best English translation. In 1884 he wrote, "We have had ten thousand messages from God to our soul in the very words of our English (King James Version) Bible; and we have prayed over and preached about the precepts and promises it enshrines, till we feel a vested interest in the volume as it is."[27] And in a famous passage that praised John Bunyan's biblical vocabulary, Spurgeon put in a parenthetical statement about "our Authorized Version, which will never be bettered, as I judge, till Christ shall come."[28]

Charles Hodge (1797–1878) was a towering American theologian of the nineteenth century. During his teaching and writing career at Princeton Seminary he produced a voluminous body of theological writing. Perhaps his signature work is his three-volume *Systematic Theology*. In that magisterial work, once Hodge gets beyond the theoretic opening material and starts to add biblical quotations to his theologizing, we are at once immersed in the world of the KJV: "Holy men spake as they were moved by the Holy Ghost" (2 Pet. 1:21); "He that knoweth God, heareth us" (1 John 4:6). Hodge argued on the floor of the Presbyterian General Assembly that the King James Bible should be retained unchanged in the publications of the American Bible Society.[29]

The Bible commentary authored by Matthew Henry (published ca. 1710) was the most widely used Bible commentary of

"The Psalmist makes it the characteristic of a good man, that he meditates on God's law day and night. And this book of the law, (says God to Joshua) shall not go out of thy mouth, but thou shalt meditate therein day and night; for then thou shalt make thy way prosperous, and thou shalt have good success." —George Whitefield, excerpt from sermon entitled "The Duty of Searching the Scriptures," showing Whitefield's use of the KJV

"And they that be wise shall shine as the brightness of the firmament; and they that turn many to righteousness as the stars for ever and ever (Daniel 12:3)." —Excerpt from sermon by D. L. Moody entitled "The Qualifications for Soul Winning," showing Moody's use of the KJV

English-speaking Protestantism for nearly three centuries. Beginning in the last quarter of the twentieth century, the author of any Bible commentary has clarified in the prefatory part of the book what English translation has been used, and in the commentary itself multiple English versions are likely to be referenced. But for over two centuries, starting around the time of Matthew Henry's commentary, it was so axiomatic that the English translation used in a commentary was the KJV that one will look in vain for any identification of the English Bible used by the author of the commentary. Matthew Henry's commentary is an early example.

Billy Graham will provide my final snapshot. One source estimates that Billy Graham has preached to live audiences totaling over two hundred million, and some of his individual televised crusades have aired to more than two million. His combined lifetime audience, including radio and television broadcasts, has been estimated to be over two billion. What English Bible did all those listeners hear? Anyone who has heard Billy Graham knows the answer to that: from the start of his evangelistic career to the end, Billy Graham held the King James Bible in his hand as he preached. I suspect that many contemporary television viewers, accustomed as they are to modern translations, are slightly jolted when they tune into a rebroadcast of a Graham crusade and hear the KJV repeatedly referenced from the pulpit.

Summary

The kaleidoscope of individual pieces that have converged in this chapter are a many-splendored testimony to the pervasiveness of the King James Bible in Britain and America. In the development of the English language, in English-speaking subcultures of non-Western countries, in the lives of Christians individually and corporately, in education, and in religious discourse, the King James Bible was the omnipresent framework for the English-speaking world for approximately three centuries.

Further Reading

David L. Barr and Nicholas Piediscalzi, eds., *The Bible in American Education* (1982).

Christopher Hill, *The English Bible and the Seventeenth-Century Revolution* (1993).

David Daniell, *The Bible in English: Its History and Influence* (2003).

7

THE INFLUENCE OF THE KING
JAMES BIBLE ON CULTURE

*When the President of the United States raises his right hand to
take the most solemn oath of office, he places his left hand on the
most sacred book for Americans: the Bible. . . . Place names . . .
repeat from coast to coast a scriptural refrain. . . . [The Bible]
flavored the common man's speech, inspired the artist's brush,
determined the poet's imagery, bestowed purpose upon a people.
It is the book.*

—EDWIN S. GAUSTAD, *A Religious History of America*

AS IN THE PRECEDING CHAPTER, I will show the influence
of the King James Bible on culture by means of random snapshots.
Just as in old family photographs the random details like a piece
of furniture or a picture hanging on the wall can give a better
sense of the life that was lived than the posed group gives, so too
a partly random survey of instances gives an accurate picture of
how the King James Bible made its presence felt in the life of the
English-speaking world.

The Courts

One index to the cultural prominence of the King James Bible is its presence in speeches, orations, and public declarations. One category is judicial. The well-established indebtedness of the English and American legal systems to biblical principles is not based on any specific Bible. Nonetheless, it is possible to show the link between the courtroom and the King James Version during the centuries of its ascendancy.

Courtroom speeches collected in a book entitled *Classics of the Bar* can give us a taste of how the KJV influence worked.[1] Here is a sampling:

- "Though hand join in hand, the wicked shall not be unpunished, but the seed of the righteous shall be delivered" (Prov. 11:21). —Benjamin Tracy, conclusion in *Tilton v. Beecher*, 1875
- "While some may not know, millions do know, that their Redeemer liveth. It is too late to argue against the teachings of Him who said: 'This day thou shalt be with me in paradise.'" —Senator William Borah, summation in the Haywood trial, 1907
- "Have ye forgotten the words of Jehovah, when upon the return from Egypt He said: 'Ye shall not afflict a fatherless child. I will surely hear that cry, and I will kill you with the sword and your wives shall be widows and your children fatherless'?" (Ex. 22:22–24). —Delphin Delmas, address to the jury in the case of the tragedy of Madison Square Garden, 1907
- "The patriarch and his family . . . were led by Jehovah out from among their enemies, up into Bethel, a place of safety. 'And they journeyed; and the terror of God was upon the cities that were round about them, and they did not pursue after the sons of Jacob' [Gen. 35:5]. They were thus protected, not prosecuted." —Senator Daniel Voorhees, address to the jury in the vindication of Crawford Black, 1871

The King James Bible's presence in judiciary circles received a blow at the dawn of the twenty-first century. By way of background, in the 1950s, movie director Cecil B. De Mille of *The Ten Commandments* fame participated with the Fraternal Order of Eagles to place the Ten Commandments in the KJV on monuments in public places throughout the United States.[2] As the United States moved into a post-Christian era, the presence of the Decalogue in courtrooms became a litigious issue. In one southern county seat after another, inscriptions of the Ten Commandments came toppling down as state courts mandated their removal from courthouses and courtrooms. The newspaper articles surrounding the controversy are readily available online, and they show that in a few cases the King James Decalogue still stands on state properties.

The removal of engraved inscriptions of the Ten Commandments hardly signaled the end of the King James Bible from civil courts, however. A 2005 article in the *New York City Law Review* adduced dozens of examples in proof of the thesis that "citations from the King James version of the Bible are numerous" in judicial opinions handed down in court to the present day.[3]

Political Discourse

Another sphere in which the King James Bible ruled supreme for over three centuries was the world of what is metaphorically called "the public square." Intellectual exchange in the public arena occurs by way of newspapers, magazines, speeches, and news coverage. The "slice of the pie" that I have chosen is speeches and communiqués by dominant political leaders.

George Washington, "America's father," made frequent reference to the Bible in his writings and addresses. Peter Lillback has produced a twenty-page tabulation of 250 biblical allusions in the writings and papers of Washington, accompanied by the verse in the King James Bible that most closely corresponds to each.[4] Here are specimens: "worse than an infidel"; "vine and fig tree" ("Washington's favorite biblical image," according to Lillback); "do justice, love mercy"; "house divided"; "cup of blessing"; "Father of lights." In a letter that Washington sent to the governors of the states on June 14, 1783, the president referenced three famous Bible verses in just one part of a long sentence: ". . . that [God] would incline the hearts of the citizens . . . to entertain a brotherly affection and love for one another, . . . and finally that he would most graciously be pleased to dispose us all to do justice, to love mercy . . ." (see Rom. 12:10; Heb. 13:1; Mic. 6:8).

Abraham Lincoln's speeches show a continuous influence of the King James Bible by way of either stylistic effects or direct quotation. A biographer claims that Lincoln's "speeches and public documents were littered with biblical allusions."[5] There is no better illustration than Lincoln's ten-sentence Gettysburg Address. In fact, someone has written a whole book on the indebtedness of Lincoln's address to the King James Bible and Book of Common Prayer.[6] The author finds dozens of biblical echoes in Lincoln's speech and concludes that "what gives Lincoln's language its distinctive flavor is . . . that it is overwhelmingly biblical, with 269 of its 272 words appearing in some form in the King James."[7]

The opening clause of the speech will suffice to illustrate how the King James Bible is present: "Four score and seven years ago our fathers brought forth upon this continent a new nation, conceived in liberty . . . ." The formula *threescore* and *fourscore* occurs dozens of times in the KJV, with Psalm 90:10 coming closest to Lincoln's opening phrase: "The days of our years are threescore years and ten." Lincoln's vocabulary of *conceived* and *brought forth* come from Old Testament messianic prophecies and the nativity story in the Gospels. And to refer to national forbears as *fathers* is to use an Old Testament idiom.

British Prime Minister Winston Churchill (1874–1965) came at the end of the era of the KJV as the unchallenged English Bible for use in political discourse. Some of Churchill's great speeches of World War II kept the King James Bible alive in his nation's active vocabulary. On Trinity Sunday, May 19, 1940, Churchill inspired his nation with a speech that ended with quotations

The King James Bible has of course been the favorite of American Presidents. In a brief address at the lighting of the Christmas tree on the White House grounds on December 24, 1945, President Truman directly quoted the following verses: "Glory to God in the highest, and on earth peace, good will toward men" (Luke 2:14). "A new commandment I give unto you, that ye love one another" (John 13:34). "They shall beat their swords into plowshares and their spears into pruning-hooks: nation shall not lift up sword against nation, neither shall they learn war any more" (Isa. 2:4).

from the KJV: "Centuries ago words were written to be a call and a spur to the faithful servants of Truth and Justice: 'Arm yourselves, and be ye men of valour, and be in readiness for the conflict; for it is better for us to perish in battle than to look upon the outrage of our nation and our altar. . . .'" The main biblical text is the KJV Apocrypha (1 Maccabees 3:58, somewhat loosely quoted by Churchill), but other KJV passages also converge. The epithet "man of valour" is a common Old Testament formula (e.g., Judg. 6:12; 11:1; 1 Kings 11:28). "Faithful servants" takes us to Matthew 24:45 and 25:21. More generally, the vocabulary reminds us of the King James style.

Near the end of a famous address in the House of Commons after Prime Minister Chamberlain had assented to the Munich Agreement, Churchill quoted Daniel 5:27 from memory in approximately its KJV form: "Thou art weighted in the balance and found wanting."[8] Another of Churchill's wartime addresses ends with the statement, "The day will come . . . when victorious nations . . . will plan and build in justice, in tradition, and in freedom, a house of many mansions where there will be room for all."[9] In yet another address, Churchill stated, "At that time I ventured to draw General Wafell's attention to the seventh chapter of the Gospel of St. Matthew, at the seventh verse, where, as you all know—or ought to know—it is written: 'Ask, and it shall be given; seek, and ye shall find; knock, and it shall be opened unto you.'"[10] *As you all know or ought to know*: it is a quick glimpse into the degree to which for three centuries most English and American citizens were totally familiar with the KJV.

The presence of the King James Bible was not limited to the formal speeches and proclamations of prime ministers and presidents. Speeches on the floor of the US Congress, for example, were until recently laced with King James formulas and allusions, and sometimes biblical references still occur. As recently as July 19, 2007, Senator Robert Byrd said in a speech from the floor of the Senate, "The Book of Proverbs in the Holy Bible, the King James Bible, tells us a righteous man regardeth the life of his beast but the tender mercies of the wicked are cruel."[11] Three years earlier Zell Miller stood in the same place and said in a speech, "The Book of Amos, as if he were speaking to us today: That the days will come, sayeth the Lord God, that I will send a famine in the land. Not a famine of bread, nor a thirst for water, but of hearing the word of the Lord."[12]

The most famous referencing of the King James Bible by an orator in modern times is Martin Luther King's "I have a dream" speech, delivered on August 28, 1963, from the steps of the Lincoln Memorial. It is easy to surmise from the title by which the speech is known—"I Have a Dream"—that King intended an allusion to Moses on Mount Pisgah, viewing the Promised Land. Actually, King does not explicitly refer to either Moses or a promised land. (King did, however, reference Moses and the Promised Land in the speech he delivered the night before his assassination.) Nonetheless, the King James Bible lives on in this speech, partly in the elevated style and affective undertow of the speech, and partly in explicit allusions. Amos 5:24 is present as King declaims, "We will not be satisfied until justice rolls down like waters and righteousness like a mighty stream." Isaiah 40:4–5 asserts its presence with the statement, "I have a dream that every valley shall be exalted, every hill and mountain shall be made low, the rough places will be made plain, and the crooked places will be made straight, and the glory of the Lord shall be revealed, and all flesh shall see it together."

Public Inscriptions

Another testimony to the ubiquitous presence of the King James Bible over the centuries is the prevalence of inscriptions in public places. These inscriptions tell a double story. They prove that the KJV was sufficiently dominant as a cultural presence to be elevated to the status of public icon. And once inscriptions were in place, they kept the KJV alive in people's consciousness and vocabulary every time they saw the inscriptions.

Whenever I step out of the dining hall at St. Anne's College, Oxford, England, I can look up at the library (formerly the administration building) and see the following inscription in stone stretching horizontally just under the roof line: "Get knowledge. Get riches. But with all thy getting, get understanding." Whenever I see the inscription, I think *King James Bible*. It turns out that this inscription is a mosaic of three separate verses from the KJV—Proverbs 18:15, Jeremiah 17:11, and Proverbs 4:7.

The King James Bible is alive and well at the United Nations headquarters in New York City. The most celebrated instance can be found across the street from the main building. It is called "the Isaiah wall" and contains these words from Isaiah 2:4: "They shall beat their swords into plowshares, and their spears into pruning hooks: nation shall not lift up sword against nation, neither shall they learn war any more." The same verse is inscribed on the base of a statue that stands on the actual grounds of the UN headquarters.

If we move back in American history, the icon of the Liberty Bell in Philadelphia gives us a notable confirmation of the hold that the King James Bible has had on the national consciousness. The famed cracked bell contains the following inscription from Leviticus 25:10: "Proclaim LIBERTY throughout all the Land unto all the Inhabitants thereof." Every year two million visitors read the verse.

Through the centuries the walls of many English churches have been decorated with Bible verses. While this practice predates the King James Bible, the sheer longevity of the KJV has meant that there are more King James Bible inscriptions in English churches than any other Bible version. The most famous modern example of church inscriptions is the eight Tablets of the Word at Coventry Cathedral (dedicated 1956). The tablets are mounted on the two side walls of the nave. Each one contains a famous statement that Jesus made about himself. A look at just one of the inscriptions immediately tells a viewer that the King James Bible was chosen for the project: "Come unto me all ye that labour and are heavy laden and I will give you rest."

A variant of public inscriptions is famous moments in history that were rendered immortal by quotations from the KJV. A selection of examples memorialized on the walls of the Dunham Bible Museum on the campus of Houston Baptist University are the following:

- "Except the Lord build the house, they labour in vain that build it" (Ps. 127:1). —Benjamin Franklin during a debate at the drafting of the US Constitution
- "What hath God wrought" (Num. 23:23). —Samuel Morse, sending the first words over his newly invented telegraph machine
- "When I consider thy heavens, the work of thy fingers, the moon and the stars, which thou hast ordained . . ." (Ps. 8:3). —Astronaut Buzz Aldrin on a television broadcast from space after his 1969 space walk
- "A house divided against itself cannot stand" (Mark 3:25). —Abraham Lincoln, acceptance speech for candidacy for the US Senate

Inscriptions on tombstones are a good index to Christian piety in England and America through the centuries. They tell the same story that I have been tracing: when English-speaking people wished to inscribe the Bible as a public declaration, the King James Bible was the translation of choice. A stroll through the Iowa cemetery where my family members and acquaintances lie buried is a trip through famous King James resurrection verses: "The LORD is my light and my salvation" (Ps. 27:1). "I am the resurrection and the life" (John 11:25). "Blessed are the dead which die in the Lord . . . , that they may rest from their labours, and their works do follow them" (Rev. 14:13). "Asleep in Jesus" (allusion to 1 Thess. 4:14). "I know that my redeemer liveth" (Job 19:25). All of these verses—and more besides—were chosen and inscribed when the KJV was the only Bible that Protestants used.

The King James Version has remained dominant in African-American circles to the present day. A well-known African Study Bible was published in 1993, when a modern translation might have been expected to be used, but the translation chosen is none other than the familiar KJV. It is perhaps no wonder that the central monument at the Civil Rights Memorial in Montgomery, Alabama, bears a Bible verse from Amos 5:24 that more closely resembles the KJV than other translations: ". . . until justice rolls down like waters and righteousness like a mighty stream."

The gate of Harvard University bears the inscription, "Open ye the gates that the righteous nation which keepeth the truth may enter." This is Isaiah 26:2, straight from the KJV. Engraved in stone on the outside of Emerson Hall at Harvard University is Psalm 8:4: "What is man that thou art mindful of him?" In instances like these, the King James Bible is a leading means by which the Christian faith continues to assert its presence in institutions that began as Christian but have long since been secularized. But KJV inscriptions do not appear only at universities that were originally Christian. During my years at the University of Oregon, I could see an engraving of the following verse at the entrance to the library: "Ye shall know the truth, and the truth shall make you free" (John 8:32).

I will note in closing an unexpected way in which a survey of public inscriptions leads to the King James Bible. "The academy" (i.e., the world of colleges and universities) has often signaled its classical roots by resorting to the Latin language when formulating its mottos and inscriptions. But in written documents, the academy often translates the Latin Bible mottos into English, and when it does so, it tends to use the KJV for biblical quotations. For example, the arch over the doorway to the famous Cavendish Laboratory of Cambridge University, England, is engraved with

Psalm 111:2 in Latin. But in one Web site after another, and in speeches that I have read on Christianity and science, the verse is quoted in its KJV form: "The works of the LORD are great: sought out of all them that have pleasure therein." This was so firmly entrenched in my mind that when I stood on the actual site, I was surprised to find the verse in Latin. The verse transmigrated from the original Cavendish Laboratory to the new one, where it appears in a form that matches the KJV (as well as the Coverdale version).

It is well documented that the Bible itself, apart from specific English translations of it, has been the major influence in English and American culture in such spheres as education, science, civil rights, and politics. This is not a story of King James influence per se. But if we find King James inscriptions on the gateway to a university, on the arch over the doorway to a world-famous science laboratory, in the lobby of a courthouse, and in a museum, these inscriptions give us glimpses into how the King James Bible was the perceived vehicle by which the Bible entered these spheres of society over a span of four centuries.

Music

Every Christmas season, selections from Handel's oratorio *The Messiah* are performed and listened to all over the English-speaking world. Every time *The Messiah* is performed, the King James Bible lives on as a cultural influence. In fact, some passages of the King James Bible owe their familiarity more to *The Messiah* than to the KJV itself.

The libretto of *The Messiah* consists of passages quoted directly from the KJV and arranged according to the chronological order of messianic history. The oratorio thus begins with Old Testament prophecies regarding the Messiah. The first words are Isaiah 40:1–3, sung by a tenor voice and beginning, "Comfort ye, comfort ye, my people, saith your God." Then a tenor sings Isaiah 40:4: "Ev'ry valley shall be exalted, and ev'ry mountain and hill made low; the crooked straight and the rough places plain." We eventually reach the nativity: "There were shepherds abiding in the field, keeping watch over their flocks by night" (Luke 2:8). And then a soprano voice sings, "And lo, the angel of the Lord came upon them, and the glory of the Lord shone round about them, and they were sore afraid" (Luke 2:9). Everything is coming straight from the King James Bible.

Almost as famous are the biblical oratorios of Felix Mendelssohn. His *Elijah* (1846) does not follow the KJV continuously as Handel's *Messiah* does, but the King James forms the skeleton on which Mendelssohn built his oratorio. The KJV is present from the opening song: "As God the Lord of Israel liveth, before whom I stand: There shall not be dew nor rain these years, but according to my word" (1 Kings 17:1). Shortly thereafter a choral passage closely resembles Exodus 20:5: "For He, the Lord our God, He is a jealous God, and He visiteth all the fathers' sins on the children to the third and the fourth generation of them that hate Him." An expert on the history of oratorio asserts that

> both Mendelssohn and Bartholomew (the English translator of the originally German libretto) wanted the translation to follow the King James version of the Bible wherever possible, and their correspondence . . . shows the extreme care they took with it and with the necessary adjustments to make the music fit the [KJV].[13]

Franz Josef Haydn's *The Creation* (1798) is also in the tradition of great biblically based oratorios. It is rooted in the Bible and Milton's epic *Paradise Lost*, but it does not generally quote either source verbatim. The question naturally arises as to which English Bible the composer of the libretto studied day by day. As so often in the material that I cover in this book, we need to begin with the assumption that unless we have evidence to the contrary, any work composed between 1700 and 1950 is based on the King James Bible. Additionally, most listeners through the years and even today probably assimilate the following famous chorus as coming from the KJV, even though it is not a verbatim quotation: "The heavens are telling the glory of God; / The firmament displays / The wonder of his works." There are enough direct biblical quotations scattered throughout the oratorio to leave us in no doubt as to which English translation the composer had before him. An example is the very opening of the oratorio, taken straight from the KJV: "In the beginning God created the heaven and the earth. And the earth was without form, and void; and darkness was upon the face of the deep."

Oratorios of course provide the most obvious opportunity for composers to incorporate the actual biblical text into their works, but other musical genres also lend themselves to it. A dip into the text of the vespers piece *Blessed Is the Man* by Sergey Rachmaninoff (1873–1943) is like a walk through the King James Bible: "Bless the Lord, O my soul. . . . O Lord my God, thou art very great. . . . Thou art clothed with honour and majesty" (Ps. 104:1). "Blessed is the man who walks not in the counsel of the wicked" (Ps. 1:1). "Lord, now lettest thou thy servant depart in peace, according to thy word" (Luke 2:29). "Blessed art thou among women" (Luke 1:28).

Even among modern choral composers who do not predominantly link their compositions to the English Bible, the King James Bible keeps showing up. We can see this partly in the titles of compositions, with the result that people perusing lists of choral music or programs of concerts will find familiar King James lines kept alive in their active vocabulary. Here is a list of random examples: "In the Beginning," by Aaron Copland (based on KJV Gen. 1:1–2:7); "I Will Lift Up Mine Eyes," by John Rutter; "Sing Ye to the Lord," by Edward Bairstow; "Lord, Thou Hast Been Our Refuge" and "O Clap Your Hands," by Ralph Vaughan Williams; "If Ye Love Me," by Thomas Tallis; "God So Loved the World," by John Stainer.

When we come to hymnody, the picture changes in a direction that I will note later in this book in reference to literature. Hymn writers, like poets, refer to and draw from the Bible without usually quoting it directly. Before we can link their texts with the King James Bible, we need to know that they used the KJV in their daily lives. Once we determine that, however, we have warrant to think of the King James Bible when we read or sing their texts.

Stanza 1 of "Great Is Thy Faithfulness"	Corresponding KJV Sources
Great is thy faithfulness, O God my Father.	Great is thy faithfulness (Lam. 3:23).
There is no shadow of turning with thee.	. . . neither shadow of turning (James 1:17).
Thou changest not	I am the LORD, I change not (Mal. 3:6).
Thy compassions they fail not.	. . . his compassions fail not (Lam. 3:22).
As Thou hast been Thou forever wilt be.	LORD, thou hast been our dwelling place in all generations (Ps. 90:1).

Isaac Watts (1674–1748) can serve as our example. Watts's vocation was that of preacher, and writing hymns was his avocation. A look at Watts's collected sermons shows at once that his English Bible was the KJV. His tombstone in Bunhill Fields, London, includes as part of its inscription Colossians 3:4: "When Christ who is our life shall appear, I shall also appear with Him in glory." With that as a context, King James associations spring up continuously as we read and sing the hymns that Watts wrote (he wrote approximately 750). Watts's hymns stand at varying degrees from the biblical text itself. "O God, Our Help in Ages Past" stands close to the text of Psalm 90. "Lord thou hast been our dwelling place in all generations," the psalm begins. "O God, our help in ages past," Watts's hymn begins, and "Our hope for years to come" is the second line of the hymn, echoing Psalm 90:14: "That we may be glad all our days." "Before the mountains were brought forth" (v. 2) finds its counterpart in "Before the hills in order stood." And these are only the beginning of parallels.

It is hard to imagine what the tradition of English and American sacred music would look like without the King James Bible as a source. A mighty stream has flowed from the KJV in our musical history.

111

The Visual Arts

With the visual arts it is even harder to link individual works with the King James Bible specifically. We have warrant for making the connection, though, if we can find evidence beyond the paintings that an artist's biblical imagination was fed by the KJV. There are enough examples of this to make big claims for the influence of the KJV on English and American painting.

We can start with a stellar example—the famous painting by Victorian painter Holman Hunt titled "The Light of the World." There are actually two originals of this painting—the first one hanging in the chapel at Keble College in Oxford and the second in St. Paul's Cathedral in London. (Hunt made the second painting because the first one was ill kept, exposed to leaking pipes, at Keble College.) The painting pictures Christ standing outside a weed-overgrown door without a handle as the morning star rises behind him, creating a halo effect. Additionally, Christ carries a lantern, which is the second source of light in a nighttime scene. We are not left to guess what English Bible inspired the painting; the inscription is right on the frame: "Behold, I stand at the door and knock: if any man hear my voice, and open the door, I will come in to him, and will sup with him, and he with me" (Rev. 3:20). The title of the painting—"The Light of the World"—also alludes to Jesus' declaration, "I am the light of the world" (John 8:12; 9:5).

In his autobiography, Hunt sometimes links particular biblical paintings with verses in the King James Bible. He links "The Light of the World" with Psalm 119:105: "Thy word is a lamp unto my feet, and light unto my path."[14] Hunt quotes John 13:4 in connection with "Christ Washing Peter's Feet."[15] Proverbs 25:20 is linked with "The Awakened Conscience": "As he that taketh away a garment in cold weather, so is he that sings songs to a heavy heart."[16] Hunt's greatest biblical painting, after "The Light of the World," is "The Finding of the Saviour in the Temple." On an ivory slip between picture and frame are the following words from Luke 2:48–49 (KJV): "and his mother said unto him, Son, why hast thou thus dealt with us? behold thy father and I have sought thee sorrowing. And he said unto them, How is it that ye sought me? whist ye not that I must be about my Father's business?"

> "If by some strange and terrible catastrophe every one of [the Continental] paintings should be blotted out, the life of Christ would still remain skillfully and beautifully portrayed by British and American artists." —Ruth Foss and Frank G. Lankard, *The English Bible and British and American Art*

American painter Thomas Cole (1801–1848) belonged to the Hudson School of landscape painters, but he also painted biblical subjects. One of them is "Hagar in the Wilderness," based on Genesis 21:14–21. No artist can paint a detailed picture of a biblical event without having pored over the biblical text. But which translation? In his correspondence Cole explains his painting of Hagar, and while he does not quote directly from the KJV, parts of the passage show a close correspondence with the KJV. Cole encloses the phrase "ready to perish" within quotation marks; it is a King James phrase from elsewhere in the Bible (multiple references).[17] Cole also puts the phrase "at the distance of a bow shot" in quotation marks, another reference to the King James text. With the King James Bible a known context for Cole's painting, we can see the presence of the KJV in other biblical paintings, especially his biblical landscape paintings, which are perhaps his signature genre.

British romanticist William Blake (1757–1827) was both a poet and artist. His lithographs on biblical subjects are among the most visible icons in college textbooks on literature and art. For a specimen of the whole, we can consider Blake's twenty-one engravings that illustrate scenes from the book of Job. Each engraving is accompanied by a text from the Bible, and it is obvious at once that Blake is quoting from the KJV.[18] For example, the inscription for plate 14 is, "When the morning stars sang together, and all the sons of God shouted for joy" (Job 38:7). Every time the biblical prints of Blake are put before a college class, the King James Bible is there, too.

The work of American Quaker painter Edward Hicks (1780–1849) is saturated with biblical resonances. His preoccupation was the peaceable kingdom motif from Isaiah's prophecy. In fact, Hicks painted it as many as a hundred times. We are not left to guess what English version of the Bible Hicks used: sometimes the King James rendition of Isaiah 11:6 appears on the frame of the paintings: "The wolf also shall dwell with the lamb, and the leopard shall lie down with the kid; and the calf and the young lion and the fatling together; and a little child shall lead them." Hicks's "Noah's Ark" is also a famous icon of American folk art.

Summary

Claims that the King James Bible was the most important influence on English and American culture for over three centuries are accurate. This is partly camouflaged because discussions of the influence of the Bible on culture are couched in terms of the generic "Bible," without recourse to what Bible is in view. But between 1700 and 1975, any consideration of biblical influence on public life, politics, education, music, and art is actually a consideration of the King James Bible.

Further Reading

Ruth Foss and Frank G. Lankard, *The English Bible and British and American Art* (1935).

Dee Dyas and Esther Hughes, *The Bible in Western Culture* (2005).

John F. A. Sawyer, ed., *The Blackwell Companion to the Bible and Culture* (2006).

A. E. Elmore, *Lincoln's Gettysburg Address: Echoes of the Bible and Book of Common Prayer* (2009); excellent on the KJV as well as on Lincoln.

PART THREE

The King James Bible
as a Literary Masterpiece

8

WHAT MAKES
AN ENGLISH BIBLE LITERARY?

*Aiming at truth, [the King James translators] achieved what later
generations recognized as beauty and elegance.*

—ALISTER MCGRATH, *In the Beginning*

A CONSIDERATION OF THE LITERARY MERITS of the King
James Bible ought to be an occasion for celebration, but in fact it
is a source of controversy. When the NIV translation of the Bible
appeared in 1978, I wrote an assessment of its literary merit for
Christianity Today. Subsequently the magazine carried a letter
to the editor chastising the magazine for devoting two pages to
a consideration of the literary merit of a Bible translation. The
writer of the letter questioned whether "literary value is any concern of God's or should be a concern of ours, in his Word."[1]

It would be wrong to dismiss this as an unenlightened view
held only by a fringe element. Debunkers of the King James Bible
regularly make the literary excellence of the KJV a mark against
it. Additionally, a great divide exists between modern translations

in the King James tradition and dynamic equivalent translations in regard to literary considerations. Translators in the King James tradition are likely to make claims for the literary excellence of their translations, whereas translators in the dynamic equivalent camp rarely make such claims. A little reflection will suggest why this is true.

As I look back on my four-decade career as a spokesperson for the literary approach to the Bible, I sometimes ponder whether I would have had that career if I had not had access to the King James tradition of English Bible translation. My conclusion is that dynamic equivalent translations, starting with the NIV, would have made my career in the Bible-as-literature movement impossible. Clearly there is more than meets the eye in regard to this subject.

The two chapters that follow this one will demonstrate the literary qualities of the King James Bible. In the present chapter I will provide an anatomy of the issues that underlie the subject. To give shape to my discussion, I will answer five questions:

1. Why is the literary aspect of an English Bible important?
2. How can we tell if an English translation is a good literary translation?
3. What has been the verdict of the general public regarding the literary merits of the King James Bible? (Chapter 11 will trace the verdict of literary authors and scholars regarding the KJV.)
4. What is there about the King James Bible that might make its literary excellence unlikely?
5. What factors explain why the literary excellence of the King James Bible is not such a surprise after all?

The Literary Nature of the Bible Itself

We need to push the subject back a step from the English Bible to the Bible in its original form. In its external form, the Bible is a literary anthology—a collection of separate books and works composed by numerous authors over a long period of time. The individual works that make up this anthology meet three primary criteria that characterize literature as a form of writing.

> "There is . . . a sense in which the Bible, since it is after all literature, cannot properly be read except as literature, and the different parts of it as the different sorts of literature they are." —C. S. Lewis, *Reflections on the Psalms*

The most customary way of defining literature is by its genres (types of writing). The two main genres of literature and of the Bible are narrative and poetry. Both of these, in turn, encompass numerous subtypes, such as hero story, tragedy, nature poem, and lyric. Even though narrative and poetry are the big categories of literature, other genres are extremely important—satire, prophecy, visionary writing, epistle, drama, oratory, and others. If the Bible is made up of literary genres almost completely, it stands to reason that an adequate English translation imports this quality from the original into the translation. Additionally, it would be wrong to conclude that English translations automatically exhibit the qualities of the genres of the original, because some do not.

Literature also advertises its distinctiveness at the level of content. Whereas expository writing primarily conveys ideas and information, literature presents human experience in such a way that we relive an experience as we read. The ever-present motto in high school and college writing courses is that the task of literary writing is to "show rather than tell." To achieve that task, language needs to be concrete and vivid rather than abstract.

A third trait of literature falls into the category of style. Style has to do with *how* writers express their content, rather than the content itself. Style, moreover, implies conscious use and manipulation of the resources of expression by an author. Even though style is an amorphous category, we can name some of its ingredients. Style begins with vocabulary. It includes syntax (sentence construction) and phraseology. It also encompasses arrangement of material (for example, patterns of repetition and balance). Finally, style includes rhetorical devices like figurative language, aphoristic effect, and uses of conventional formulas (such as epithets to name persons or things, or the attention-getting "behold" before an utterance).

When Does an English Translation Rise to the Status of Literature?

On the day on which I introduce literary prose in my literature courses, I circulate a handout containing famous prose passages that everyone would label as literary—the opening paragraph of the Gettysburg Address, a descriptive paragraph from Mark Twain's *Life on the Mississippi*, a paragraph from John Donne's "no man is an island" meditation, and such like. I then ask my students to identify what raises these passages above everyday expository prose. There is a range of answers to that question, but the constant is that there are elements in every passage of literary prose that set it apart from the expository prose with which we conduct the daily business of life.

This is true of a majority of the Bible in its original Hebrew and Greek as well. The mere fact that some of the original Bible uses common words of the day does not negate my claim. The relevant question is what biblical writers do *with* the common vocabulary of their day. We can see this principle at work most clearly in the poetry of the Bible. Poetry advertises its distinctiveness first by being written in verse form (parallelism, in the case of the Bible), and second by its reliance on imagery and figurative language (the "poetic idiom," as literary critics call it). Poetry never sounds like everyday prose, even when its vocabulary resembles that of ordinary speech. Approximately half of the Bible is written in poetic form (broadly defined to include figurative language as well as poetry written in verse form).

We need to note an unbridgeable gap between advocates of a conversation-style Bible translation and the work of modern biblical scholars. The moment we pick up a scholarly Bible commentary or journal article dealing with a Bible passage, it is apparent that modern scholars find artistry and intricacy of

> The idea of the Bible-as-literature can be traced back to the Bible itself. The writer of Ecclesiastes gives us a self-portrait of the writer as a self-conscious composer, very interested in form and style as well as content: "Besides being wise, the Preacher also taught the people knowledge, weighing and studying and arranging many proverbs with great care. The Preacher sought to find words of delight, and uprightly he wrote words of truth" (Eccles. 12:9–10, ESV).

effect everywhere in the Bible. These same scholars have documented the extensive degree to which the literary genres that we find in the Bible have parallels in the literature (not the marketplace conversation) of the biblical authors' surrounding cultures. Claims that the Bible in its original form was unliterary are an illusion.

We can say summarily that the ultimate touchstone by which we can recognize literature is that it deviates positively from everyday discourse. Everyday expository discourse seeks to be transparent: it does not call attention to itself but exists to move a reader or listener as directly as possible to a body of information. By contrast, literature consistently draws attention to itself. With literature we are continuously aware that the author is doing things with language and discourse that we do not do in ordinary discourse. Advocates of modern colloquial Bible translations want the Bible to sound like the newspaper and conversation at the bus stop. Literature always has properties that remove it from those types of discourse.

With that as the starting point, it is readily apparent when an English Bible translation rises to the status of being literary. It is literary when it preserves the literary qualities of the Bible in its original Hebrew and Greek form. This starts with the literary genres of the Bible, most obviously with the poetry but extending to other genres as well. Second, a literary Bible retains the vividness and experiential quality of the Bible. And it culminates in the style with which the original is embodied in the English language (as I will explore in detail in chapters 9 and 10).

The King James Bible is the gold standard for a literary Bible, as posterity has correctly asserted. We should not make much of the fact that in the seventeenth century the literary excellence of the KJV was hardly mentioned. People were not thinking in terms of "the Bible as literature" but only of the Bible as God's word for life and thought. English poet George Herbert was a person of finely tuned artistic temperament, and it would be hard to find a poet who made more creative use of the English Bible in his own poetry. Yet Herbert says nothing overtly about the literary nature of the Authorized Version.[2]

But this does not necessarily mean that people were unresponsive to the literary superiority of the King James Bible from the beginning. It is unlikely that the King James Bible would have supplanted the Geneva Bible as quickly as it did if it did not have qualities that won the hearts of the faithful. Excellence of form always increases the impact of an utterance, and it stands to reason that the literary quality of the KJV was recognized even if that subject was not on people's radar screens until a century later. Furthermore, it takes a person with a literary education to recognize literary elements in a book, so we cannot expect that most readers of the KJV could articulate its literary merits.

> "For literary quality . . . the King James Bible is supreme among the English translations. This has been stated so often, and men of all ranks have been so eager to affirm it, that it would be tedious to attempt a review of so great a mass of testimony." —Charles C. Butterworth, *The Literary Lineage of the King James Bible, 1340–1611*

Even if we exempt the literary experts whom I will survey in chapter 11, the accolades for the literary merit of the KJV have been striking. *McGuffey's Fifth Eclectic Reader*, while not designating the KJV or using the word *literature*, nonetheless implied as much when it called the Bible "the best of classics the world has ever admired." John Richard Green, in his classic book *A Short History of the English People*, famously wrote that "as a mere literary monument, the English version of the Bible remains the noblest example of the English tongue."[3] Bible collector Donald Brake offers the opinion that "the King James Version is the crown jewel of English literature. . . . Its influence on the English-speaking world is as much due to the beauty of its expression as its accuracy of translation."[4] And C. Boyd McAfee believes that "from the literary point of view the [King James] Bible stands as an English classic, indeed, as the outstanding English classic."[5]

An Unlikely Occurrence?

Scholars who write about English Bible translation overwhelmingly believe that the literary excellence of the KJV is nothing short of miraculous. If we consider certain external factors, there would seem to be a basis for this verdict.

We can begin with the committee structure that produced the King James Bible. There were forty-seven translators, divided into six committees, meeting at three different locations over a span of six years. The working manuscripts were passed among all the committees. It would seem impossible that the result could be a translation that is (a) uniform and (b) literarily distinguished. The unlikelihood produced an often-quoted verdict that the KJV is the only literary masterpiece ever to have been produced by a committee.

Second, the King James translators were not literary scholars. They were mainly experts in the ancient Hebrew and Greek languages in which the Bible was written. If by an act of imagination we transport them into our own situation, they would most likely be seminary professors teaching Hebrew and Greek with special attention to the Bible.

Third, and as a result of that, the translators did not think of themselves as producing a literary Bible. Their primary aim was to produce an accurate translation of the original Bible. C. B. McAfee notes that "it was never in their minds that they were making a world literature"; for the translators, "the Bible is a book of religious significance from first to last."[6] Alister

McGrath similarly claims that "the king's translators achieved [literary merit] unintentionally, by focusing on what, to them, was a greater goal. . . . The achievement of prosaic and poetic elegance that resulted was, so to speak, a most happy accident of history."[7]

Explaining the Paradox

But if we factor in additional pieces of information, the production of a literary Bible by the King James translators seems much less of a mystery. These factors relate mainly to the cultural situation of late-sixteenth and early-seventeenth century. This was the age of the Renaissance in England, and once we say that, several things immediately follow.

The Renaissance was the great age of humanism—the striving to perfect all human possibilities in this world. Human achievement was perceived as a value. The arts, including imaginative literature, were cultivated with zest. Beauty was esteemed. This habit of mind was second nature to Renaissance people and would naturally have been operative in everything that the King James translators did.

> One of the highest compliments that the KJV received appears in the preface to the English Revised Version of 1881, where the revisers say, "We have had to study this great Version carefully and minutely, line by line; and the longer we have been engaged upon it the more we have learned to admire its simplicity, its dignity, its power, its happy turns of expression, its general accuracy, and . . . the music of its cadences, and the felicities of its rhythm."

Renaissance humanism produced a distinctive educational program. While the ultimate goal was godliness, the curriculum consisted of day-long language study in which the mastery of written and spoken Latin and Greek dominated everything. From another point of view the students were busy reading the great books from the past. Education was built around words and language, and facility with language was the natural result. The King James translators were the product of this culture, so it is not surprising that they produced an English Bible noteworthy for its style.

At the same time, the idea was gaining momentum that the Bible in its original form was a literary book. According to David Norton, John Calvin did "much to open to his successors a way of believing the Bible is supreme literature—that is, best in words and literary form as well as in content."[8] Manuals of rhetoric in England included examples from the Bible in such a way as to lead readers "to infer that the Bible is eloquent."[9] John Donne, famous as both poet and preacher, claimed in his sermons "that the books of Scripture are the eloquentest books in the world, that every word in them hath . . . weight and value."[10] This attitude toward the Bible reached its apex thirty-five years after the publication of the KJV in the Westminster Confession of Faith, which celebrated both "the heavenliness of the matter" in the Bible and "the majesty of the style" along with "many other incomparable excellencies."

The King James translators were surrounded by images of greatness as they went about their work. Their surroundings were not courtly, but they were the great buildings at Oxford and Cambridge Universities and Westminster Abbey—buildings that are among the greatest architectural feats of history. One is not likely to produce a cheap and tawdry Bible translation when walking to committee meetings amid such sublimity. Someone has written about the translators that "at Oxford and Cambridge the learned men breathed the air of noble language, amid brilliant buildings and gardens which could excite them to lofty efforts."[11]

Additionally, the English language was at a moment of great energy and expansiveness. Scholars regularly speak of a window of opportunity in which the King James translation appeared. Here are five representative statements:

> This was, after all, the period of Shakespeare, when the English language itself was at its apex. No other period in English literature

venerated the English language as did the late sixteenth and early seventeenth centuries. . . . The King James Version came along in history when the English language was in its golden age.[12]

It was a matter of extreme good fortune that the King James version came into being just when it did, for this was the period when our language reached what G. M. Trevelyan has called "its brief perfection."[13]

It can hardly be mere coincidence that the King James Bible came near the climax of a splendid epoch in English political and literary history. The English vocabulary was more capacious, the syntax more flexible and mature.[14]

The language at the period during which the Bible was being translated into English was in its most plastic stage. It was a time of intense living, of incomparable zest in life. . . . With the new quickening of every phase of life, the language itself kept even pace. There was a fresh consciousness of its possibilities, a sovereign and masterful exploitation of its hitherto undreamed resources. . . . So far as their medium was concerned, the King James translators fell upon lucky days.[15]

The King James Version was produced at the peak of a great age of literary creativity, of colossal learning, of abounding piety, and at a ripely formative period in the development of the English language. It has been hard to find another such grouping of important factors—religious, educational, literary, philological—such as helped to make the great version unique. The absence of one or more of these factors goes far to account for the comparative weakness of a certain of the efforts of those who attack the problem of a better rendering.[16]

Someone has aptly said that "a great age produced a great book."[17]

Finally—and to return to where this chapter began—the contours of any English Bible translation depend ultimately on how closely the translation remains tied to the words of the original texts of the Bible. The Bible in its original is a very literary book. This would have been enough to guarantee a literary King James Bible. David Norton claims that "the KJB and its predecessors . . . did not aim for eloquence such as the world knew it, but they did aim for precisely the kind of accuracy needed to pick up this idea of eloquence."[18] C. B. McAfee, after declaring the KJV "the greatest English classic," offers his opinion that one of the factors that "helped to determine its English style is the loyalty of the translators to the original, notably the Hebrew."[19] Reynolds Price agrees: "The power and memorability of the King James is an almost automatic result of its loyal adherence to principles of literalness and the avoidance of paraphrase."[20]

Summary

Before we speak of the King James Bible as a literary masterpiece, we also need to speak of the Bible in its original form as a literary masterpiece. The qualities that make an English Bible literary are the qualities found in the original, including the presence of literary genres, concrete human experience as the subject matter, and features of style that make it different from everyday expository discourse. While the King James translators did not use literary terminology when they spoke about the Bible, the whole cultural context in which they lived and worked make it easy to see how they produced a literary Bible.

Further Reading

Cleland Boyd McAfee, *The Greatest English Classic* (1912).
Charles C. Butterworth, *The Literary Lineage of the King James Bible, 1340–1611* (1941).
David Norton, *A History of the Bible as Literature* (1993).

9

PROSE STYLE

IN THE KING JAMES BIBLE

The noblest monument of English prose.

—JOHN LIVINGSTON LOWES on the King James Bible

IT IS TIME TO VALIDATE the extravagant claims for the literary excellence of the King James Bible that appear in the preceding chapter. There are multiple ways to organize the data; it turns out that the old standby division into prose and poetry works beautifully.

When we survey what scholars have said about what makes the King James Bible a literary masterpiece, we are immediately surrounded by a cloud of contradictory claims: The secret of the King James Version's success is its reliance on simple English words of Anglo-Saxon origin; no, it is the *exalted* vocabulary of the text that makes the KJV supreme. The thing that most characterizes the King James Bible is its simplicity; no, the KJV is a triumph of elegance and majesty. Everyone knows that the KJV is the noblest monument of English *prose*; no, the King James Bible is a *poetic* Bible, in contrast to prosaic modern translations.

Is it possible that all of the contradictory claims are partly true? Does the triumph of the King James Bible consist of its equilibrium among competing qualities? This chapter and the next will answer those questions. The only preliminary observation that I will make is that one of the great fallacies about the KJV is that it is a single thing: it is *only* simple, it is *only* elegant, and so forth. The strength of the King James Bible is actually its variety and flexibility.

The Prose Language of the King James Bible

A good starting point is the language of the Bible in its original form, especially the Hebrew Old Testament. It is a commonplace that the language of the Old Testament is overwhelmingly concrete rather than abstract. Albert C. Cook said of the Old Testament that "nearly every word presents a concrete meaning, clearly visible even through a figurative use. . . . Everywhere we are face to face with motion, activity, life."[1] In a similar vein, C. Boyd McAfee wrote, "That is the natural method of the Hebrew language—concrete, vivid, never abstract, simple in its phrasing. The King James translators are exceedingly loyal to that original."[2]

"In Hebrew, . . . the vocabulary was consciously pictorial and concrete in its character. . . . The writers of the Old Testament—and to a less degree those of the New as well—thought and felt and spoke in images—in a vocabulary compact of nearly all the physical sensations that flesh is heir to. . . . The Biblical vocabulary is compact of the primal stuff of our universal humanity—of its universal emotional, sensory experiences." —John Livingston Lowes, "The Noblest Monument of English Prose"

The opening of the story of Abraham and Sarah's hospitality shown to three angelic visitors (Gen. 18:1–5) can serve as a preliminary example of how the KJV deals with the concrete vocabulary of the original:

And the Lord appeared unto him in the plains of Mamre, and he sat in the tent door, in the heat of the day. And he lift up his eyes

130

and looked, and lo, three men stood by him: and when he saw *them*, he ran to meet them from the tent door, and bowed himself toward the ground, and said, My LORD, if now I have found favour in thy sight, pass not away, I pray thee, from thy servant. Let a little water, I pray you, be fetched, and wash your feet, and rest yourselves unto the tree, and I will fetch a morsel of bread; and comfort ye your hearts; after that you shall pass on.

The whole rural scene comes alive in our imaginations. The images are homely and concrete. The passage illustrates the spare, unembellished style that is customary in the narrative parts of the King James Bible (including the stories in the New Testament).

The second main prose genre of the Bible (in addition to narrative) is discourse, whether spoken or epistolary. The following excerpt from the Olivet Discourse (Matt. 24:29–31) can stand as a representative passage of prose discourse:

Immediately after the tribulation of those days shall the sun be darkened, and the moon shall not give her light, and the stars shall fall from heaven, and the powers of the heavens shall be shaken. And then shall appear the sign of the Son of man in heaven, and then shall the tribes of the earth mourn, and they shall see the Son of man coming in the clouds of heaven with power and great glory. And he shall send his angels with a great sound of a trumpet, and they shall gather together his elect from the four winds, from one end of heaven to the other.

This is more mixed than the story of the angelic visitors to Abraham and Sarah. Certainly the passage puts us in touch with the great primary images of human experience—sun, moon, stars, clouds, trumpet. But there are also abstract words—*tribulation*, *powers*, *sign*, *glory*, *gathering together*, *elect*.

The King James Bible does not give us a single style (concrete instead of abstract, for example). Debunkers of the KJV as well as defenders of it often seize upon half of the equation and treat it as though it were the whole equation. For those who dislike what they often call a sonorous English Bible, the presence of exalted Latin-derived words is sternly denounced. Defenders counter that by saying, Oh, no, look at the concrete vocabulary of the stories in the KJV. But in fact we cannot read very far in the narrative and discourse parts of the King James Bible to see that the style is neither predominantly abstract nor solely concrete. It is a blended style.

Were the King James translators inconsistent, then? No—they were true to the original. The vocabulary of the King James Bible is as varied as the original is.

Simple Anglo-Saxon Vocabulary

The dual tendencies already noted run parallel to a second dichotomy that regularly surfaces in discussions on the KJV. The fashion of the moment is to make large claims for the simple, monosyllabic, Anglo-Saxon vocabulary of the King James Bible. Here is a specimen statement:

> The words are short, and in general short words are the strong ones. . . . Of course, another way of saying that is that the words are generally Anglo-Saxon, and, while in the original spelling they were much longer, yet in their sound they were as brief as they are in our present spelling. There is no merit in Anglo-Saxon words except in the fact that they are concrete, definite, non-abstract words. They are words that mean the same to everybody; they are part of the common experience.[3]

The KJV "fused Anglo-Saxon and Latin elements—the Latin, as one scholar notes, parting stateliness and sonority to its diction; the Anglo-Saxon conforming to the Hebrew in homely vigor, concreteness, and directness of style." —Benson Bobrick, *Wide as the Waters*

There can be no doubt that the narrative parts of the KJV tend toward simple words, though claims of a monosyllabic norm are harder to substantiate. The following excerpt from Luke's nativity story will provide a good test case (Luke 2:7–10):

And she brought forth her first born son, and wrapped him in swaddling clothes, and laid him in a manger, because there was no room for them in the inn. And there were in the same country shepherds abiding in the field, keeping watch over their flock by night. And lo, the angel of the Lord came upon them, and the glory of the Lord shone round about them, and they were sore afraid. And the angel said unto them, Fear not, for behold, I bring you good tidings of great joy, which shall be to all people.

The prevailing style here is simple. The words are of Anglo-Saxon origin and mainly monosyllabic, as opposed to polysyllabic, Latin-derived words.

But again we need to acknowledge that not all prose in the Bible belongs to the narrative genre. In the Bible, as in everyday life, people generally rise to the level of formality that an occasion requires. One of the most solemn occasions recorded in the Bible is King Solomon's prayer at the dedication of the temple. Here is an excerpt that appears near the beginning of the prayer (1 Kings 8:27–30):

But will God indeed dwell on the earth? Behold, the heaven, and heaven of heavens, cannot contain thee: how much less this house that I have built? Yet have thou respect unto the prayer of thy servant, and to his supplication, O LORD my God, to hearken unto the cry and the prayer, which thy servant prayeth before thee today: That thine eyes may be open toward this house, night and day, *even* the place of which thou hast said, My Name shall be there. . . . And hearken thou to the supplication of thy servant, and of thy people Israel, when they shall pray towards this place: and hear in heaven thy dwelling place, and when thou hearest, forgive.

The vocabulary is predominantly Anglo-Saxon rather than Latinate. But there are formal words as well—*respect, hearken, supplication.*

To anticipate a point that I will elaborate below, vocabulary is not the only criterion that determines prose style. The vocabulary of Solomon's prayer is relatively simple, but the effect is grand.

That is because of the rhetoric with which Solomon composed his prayer. Stately epithets appear, such as: "heaven of heavens," "the place of which thou hast said," "thy servant," "heaven thy dwelling place." The passage begins with a rhetorical question. There are interspersed formal words like *indeed* and *behold* and *how much less*.

My specimen from the nativity story is at the simple end of the continuum of prose style, and Solomon's prayer of dedication is in the middle. When we move to the New Testament Epistles, we are usually at the formal end of the continuum. Here are the first five verses of Romans 5:

> Therefore being justified by faith, we have peace with God through our Lord Jesus Christ. By whom also we have access by faith into this grace wherein we stand, and rejoice in hope of the glory of God. And not only *so*, but we glory in tribulations also, knowing that tribulation worketh patience; and patience, experience; and experience, hope; and hope maketh not ashamed.

This passage has a large admixture of abstract words. Furthermore, it refutes a common claim that Paul totally repudiated rhetorical embellishment. At the end of the passage Paul uses what classical rhetoricians called *gradatio*, which we call "stairstep arrangement," in which the last key word in one phrase is repeated as the first key word in the next phrase.

Summary: The Blended Vocabulary of the King James Bible

Thus far I have discussed the vocabulary of the King James prose. It is a predominantly simple vocabulary, but there is a rather consistent subordinate thread of more abstract and exalted words woven into the verbal tapestry. John Livingston Lowes wrote that "the Biblical style is characterized not merely by homely vigour and pithiness of phrase, but also by a singular nobility of diction."[4]

Equally important is the fact that simple words do not necessarily result in a "low" or conversational style (as proponents of colloquial modern translations claim). Not much of the material

134

> "There are in the English vocabulary . . . two chief elements. . . . To its native, Saxon element it owes a homely vigour, a forthrightness and vividness and concreteness, an emotional appeal. . . . To its foreign element—chiefly the Latin component. . .—is due, among other things, a sonorousness, a stateliness, a richness of music, a capacity for delicate discrimination. . . . Now one element is predominant, now the other; more frequently there is an intimate fusion of the two." —John Livingston Lowes, "The Noblest Monument of English Prose"

that I have quoted sounded like everyday conversation even in the original text. I can imagine a reader asking, What about the dialogue between Abraham and his visitors? In keeping with the extraordinary nature of the event, Abraham speaks in a formal and stylized way: "My LORD, if now I have found favour in thy sight, pass not away, I pray thee, from thy servant" (Gen. 18:3). In this passage the King James rendition is stylized and elegant because that was how Abraham spoke the words to his guests.

Four Distinctive Stylistic Traits

What we as modern readers experience as the distinctive King James style is made up of numerous individual features. Some that strike as highly distinctive, such as the *thees* and the *thous* and the inflected verb endings (*sayest*, *givest*), were ordinary grammar in the era that produced the King James Bible. But others are rooted in the commitment of the King James translators to reproduce the original Hebrew and Greek as closely as possible. These are not Renaissance or Elizabethan traits but Hebrew and Greek traits.

One of these features slides right past us until we are alerted to it. It relates to the genitive or possessive construction. A common biblical formula is the construction noun plus the preposition *of* plus noun (noun + *of* + noun). The standard English way of achieving the same effect is to turn the second noun into a modifying adjective placed in front of the first noun. Here are examples: We would say *land animal*; Genesis 1:24 states *beast of the earth*.

We would say *iron rod*; Psalm 2:9 states *rod of iron*. We would say *strong men*; Isaiah 5:22 says *men of strength*. We would say *Samaritan woman*; John 4:7 renders it *woman of Samaria*. We would say *sky*; Genesis 1:20 states *firmament of heaven*.

A subcategory of the noun-plus-*of*-plus-noun construction occurs when the same noun appears in both halves of the formula. The effect is to suggest the quality of being superlative—the most heightened form that can be imagined—and it yields some famous King James phrases: King of Kings, Lord of Lords, Song of Songs, Holy of Holies, Vanity of Vanities.

Even when the noun-*of*-noun formula does not meet the special conditions noted in the preceding paragraphs, it is simply a common formulation in the King James Bible. Here are specimens of what can be found multiple times on most pages of the KJV: "angel of the LORD" (Ps. 34:7), "the river of God" (Ps. 65:9), "the bread of wickedness" (Prov. 4:17), "abundance of peace" (Ps. 37:11), "fruit of righteousness" (James 3:18), "idleness of the hands" (Eccles. 10:18), "words of truth" (Eccles. 12:10).

Once alerted to the noun-*of*-noun construction, we can find it nearly continuously in the King James Bible. In addition to preserving the word order of the original, the King James Bible gains rhythmic smoothness with this construction. Gerald Hammond, who has written about this with particular clarity, observes that because the King James formula (based on the original text) "is so redolent of traditional Bible English, . . . it is likely to be one of the first victims of the modern translator; and when it goes so, too, goes its rhythmic beauty."[5]

A second formula that we have come to regard as "vintage King James" are the words *lo* and *behold*. The grammatical term for them is *interjection*. They are customarily used as a lead-in to something that follows: "Behold, I stand at the door and knock" (Rev. 3:20). The function of the formula is to signal the spectacular nature of an event (e.g., "Behold, an angel of the Lord came upon him"—Acts 12:7) or the profound importance of a statement ("Lo, I am with you always"—Matt. 28:20). The effect is awe-inspiring.

Third, very similar to *lo* and *behold* is the intensifying word *verily*. Sometimes it appears by itself: "For verily I say unto you" (Matt. 5:18). Even more solemn are occasions when the word appears twice: "Verily, verily, I say unto you" (John 5:19). Whenever the word appears in the Bible, it serves notice on the listener or reader that what follows is of the highest importance, and the speaker of the highest veracity.

Finally, we cannot read far in the King James Bible without sensing a more-than-ordinary concentration of the conjunction *and*: "And Ehud put forth his left hand, and took the dagger from his right thigh, and thrust it into his belly. And the haft also went in after the blade: and the fat closed *upon* the blade, so that he could not draw the dagger out of his belly, and the dirt came out" (Judg. 3:21–22). It so happens that the ancient Hebrews and Greeks absolutely loved this conjunction translated as "and." In Hebrew the prefix *waw* (the sixth letter of the alphabet) has this meaning; in the Greek the word is *kai*.

> "To have concentrated so much on the simple word 'and' might seem to indicate an obsession with trivialities. I hope not because it is an important part of my purpose to demonstrate that what made the English Bible so powerful and influential an achievement was something begun by Tyndale and refined by his successors, namely a willingness to pay attention to the minutiae of biblical style." —Gerald Hammond, *The Making of the English Bible*

The effect of these frequent *ands* in the King James Bible is to create a tremendous sense of continuity. Everything flows in sequence. The construction often shows a sense of cause and effect, as one thing produces the next, which produces the next.

Prose Rhythm in the King James Bible

The most exalted claims about the prose style of the King James Bible focus not on vocabulary but on rhythm. Before I explore the prose rhythm of the KJV, I need to dispel the view of some that this is a technical subject that ordinary people lack the interest and ability to understand. Many people in the pew may, indeed, lack the vocabulary to understand what is happening when they hear the Bible read (or even read it silently by themselves), but they emphatically do know the difference between smooth rhythm and staccato effect when they hear passages read aloud.

Rhythm in any genre consists of the regular recurrence of a pattern of sound. Prose rhythm differs from poetic rhythm, but it is no less important. Good rhythm can be defined as a smooth flow of language—not monotonously smooth but predominantly smooth. The word *rhythm* implies a back-and-forth recurrence, the rise and fall of language. Anything that impedes the smoothness of flow is detrimental to good rhythm.

The test of prose rhythm is to read a passage aloud. While it may be useful at a certain point to analyze what makes the rhythm of a passage good or bad, we do not need analysis to know whether the rhythm is good or bad. When we bite into an apple, we know at once whether it is good or bad; when we hear twenty seconds of a prose passage, we can make a similar judgment.

In poetry, the line is the recurrent unit (as shown by the way in which poetic lines do not run all the way to the right margin of the page); syntax (arrangement of sentence elements) and phraseology are of secondary importance. In prose, where the sentence is the recurrent unit, this order is reversed.

The biggest building block in prose is the sentence. We *always* stop at the end of a sentence in both silent and oral reading. But prose rhythm is more governed by phraseology within a sentence. Phraseology is usually highlighted by punctuation marks such as commas and semicolons, but in reading a passage of prose we intuitively make pauses in addition to those indicated by punctuation marks. I will note in passing that the King James Bible of 1611 is over-punctuated by modern standards because the translators wished to aid public reading of the text. The smallest unit of prose rhythm is meter—the arrangement of stressed and unstressed syllables into a pattern of regular recurrence. At this level prose behaves much like poetry.

Smooth flow is the mark of good prose rhythm. With good rhythm, we hear the rise and fall of verbal sound in a wave-like pattern. The technical name for this rise and fall in the movement of language is *cadence*.

Nearly everyone who has written on English Bible translation agrees that the prose rhythm of the King James Bible is matchless. Almost any prose passage from the King James Bible will validate the accolades. Here is King James rhythm in a narrative passage (Mark 4:36–39, with original punctuation retained):

> And when they had sent away the multitude, they took him, even as he was in the ship, and there were also with him other little ships. And there arose a great storm of wind, and the waves beat into the ship, so that it was now full. And he was in the hinder part of the ship asleep on a pillow: and they awake him, and say unto him, Master, carest thou not, that we perish? And he arose, and rebuked the wind, and said unto the sea, Peace, be still: and the wind ceased, and there was a great calm.

This passage is "scripted" for oral reading. The retention of the Greek *kai*, translated as a coordinating conjunction *and*, is fully evident and keeps the momentum flowing. The passage is a seamless rhythmic progression. Aphoristic effect (phrases having the power of being memorable) is characteristic of the entire King James Bible, including the unembellished narratives that are a hallmark of biblical narrative style. Examples in the story of the calming of the storm include "carest thou not that we perish?"; "peace, be still"; "and there was a great calm."

Prose rhythm is as important to the discourse sections of the King James Bible as it is in the narrative sections. Here is an excerpt from the set piece of exalted King James prose, the epithalamion in praise of love in 1 Corinthians 13 (vv. 3–4, 7):

> And though I bestow all my goods to feed the poor, and though I give my body to be burned, and have not charity, it profiteth me nothing. Charity suffereth long, and is kind; charity envieth not;

charity vaunteth not itself, is not puffed up. . . ; beareth all things, believeth all things, hopeth all things, endureth all things.

The passage flows in a wave-like cadence built out of the rise and fall of sound. The passage also shows how the unaccented *eth* verb endings keep the rhythm flowing smoothly. Robbed of these unaccented endings, modern translations often bump along in staccato fashion: "always protects, always trusts, always hopes, always perseveres."

"Because the text of the King James Version was to be used at church services, the translators worked hard to make it suitable for reading aloud—its punctuation indicated emphasis and its rhythmic prose could be used to great effect. . . . The text's oral quality can also be traced to the translation process. Since each translator had to read his version aloud to the others, his work was written as language to be spoken." —*The Bible through the Ages* (*Reader's Digest* book)

An Oral Prose Style

The prose rhythm of the King James Bible leads naturally to the important related issue of orality. There are two dimensions to this topic. One is the degree to which the King James Bible is itself an oral book whose excellence shines brightest when we hear it read aloud. The second aspect is to note certain things about the culture in which the King James translators lived and translated.

The ultimate "proof of the pudding" in regard to the KJV itself is simply to read it aloud and listen to it read aloud. The testimonies of experts do not prove the point but express the tribute that we, too, naturally want to express. Charles Butterworth wrote, "The translators of the King James Bible were men of sensitive ears. They had a regard for the melody and the tempo of what they wrote. They could hear what was lovely in nearly every passage."[6] Someone else claims that "aside from the diction and phraseology, the rhythms of the King James Version, deeply rooted in emotion and stronger than in earlier English Bibles, have greatly influenced English style."[7]

The orality of the King James Bible is reinforced if we conduct a little research into the Renaissance era as an oral culture. The title page of the King James Bible claimed that this Bible was "appointed to be read in churches." This reading was oral reading. There can be no doubt that the translators had oral reading in mind as they translated. John Selden, living in the same era as the King James translators, left an account in his *Table Talk* of how the King James translators proceeded during their final committee meetings. The procedure was for the committee member of highest authority on a given part of the Bible to read the text aloud. If the translators "found any fault, they spoke up; if not, he read on."[8] Adam Nicolson writes, "This is the kingdom of the spoken. The ear is the governing organ of this prose; if it sounds right, it is right. The spoken word is the heard word, and what governs acceptability of a particular verse is not only accuracy but euphony."[9]

Summary

The prose of the King James Bible is one of its greatest triumphs. The foundation of the vocabulary is simple and concrete, enriched with exalted words and rhetoric as the original text of the Bible required. Certain stylistic traits like an abundance of "and" coordinates makes the KJV distinctive and memorable. The crowning touch on this prose style is its rhythmic excellence.

Further Reading

Albert S. Cook, *The Bible and English Prose Style* (1903).
John Livingston Lowes, "The Noblest Monument of English Prose," in *Essays in Appreciation* (1936).
Gerald Hammond, *The Making of the English Bible* (1982).

10

POETIC EFFECTS
IN THE KING JAMES BIBLE

*The closer the Bible is brought to the . . . writing the American
masses are now accustomed to, the farther it must depart from
the language of Shakespeare and Milton. This is an age of prose,
not of poetry, and [a modern translation] is a prose Bible, while
K.J.V. is a poetic one.*

—DWIGHT MACDONALD, "The Bible in Modern Undress"

IF AN ENGLISH BIBLE TRANSLATION does not make the
grade with the poetry of the Bible, it does not make the grade at
all. At least a third of the Bible is poetry. Many whole books are
poetic—Job, Psalms, Song of Solomon, and most of the prophetic
books. But the poetry of the Bible extends well beyond the poetic books of the Bible. Figurative language appears throughout
the Bible, and whenever it does, its poetic integrity needs to be
preserved in the process of translation.

The title that I have given to this chapter pushes the subject
beyond poetry per se to poetic *effects* in the King James Bible.
Just as the New Testament Epistles contain a lyric *quality* even

though they are technically not lyrics, the King James Bible as a whole possesses certain qualities that we normally consider poetic. Albert C. Cook correctly observed that "much of Hebrew prose was poetical, in the sense that it employed [poetic] devices to a greater or less extent, and all of it was poetical in the sense . . . of the [concreteness of] Hebrew vocabulary."[1]

The Poetic Idiom of the King James Bible

Poets speak a language all their own. This language goes by the common name of "the poetic idiom." The most basic element of that idiom is imagery. An image is any word that names a concrete thing or action. Poets think in images. An English Bible translation is adequate only if it leads a reader or listener to think in images as well.

In addition to images, the poetic idiom consists of figures of speech. The most important ones are metaphor or simile—comparisons or analogies. A host of additional figures of speech round out the poet's repertoire, including symbol, apostrophe, hyperbole, allusion, metonymy, and synecdoche. Most figures of speech are images at some level, so the primacy of the image in poetry remains the heart of the matter.

Because the King James translators were committed to the translation philosophy known today as verbal equivalence, it is no surprise that the poetry of the King James Bible is one of its greatest triumphs. Almost universally, the King James translators avoided the impulse of modern dynamic equivalent translators to remove figures of speech from the text or, not trusting readers to interpret poetry, to insert interpretive commentary into the text.

The best way to illustrate this is simply to quote a few random examples and briefly analyze what makes the King James translation great poetry. The opening verse of Psalm 1 is a good starting point: "Blessed is the man that walketh not in the counsel of the ungodly, nor standeth in the way of sinners, nor sitteth in the seat of the scornful." This verse has become something of a "hot potato" on the contemporary translation scene, with dynamic equivalent translations showing various degrees of nervousness about whether modern readers can handle the metaphors in the verse. The King James translators were not nervous. They retained the metaphors of a person's walking and standing on a path, and sitting in the seat, metaphoric of serving on a town council.

Here is the King James rendition of Psalm 91:4–6, part of a catalog of God's acts of protection: "He shall cover thee with his feathers, and under his wings shalt thou trust; his truth shall be *thy* shield and buckler. Thou shalt not be afraid for the terror by night, *nor* for the arrow *that* flieth by day, *nor* for the pestilence that walketh in darkness, *nor* for the destruction *that* wasteth at noonday." The poetic imagery and figurative language of the original are fully preserved.

> "What did [the KJV] bring to its own consummation? Much every way, but most in poetry and beauty—in fitness of word, fineness of shading, variety of rhythm, and grace of cadence." —Charles C. Butterworth, *The Literary Lineage of the King James Bible, 1340–1611*

The same impulse carries over to the New Testament. Jesus' Sermon on the Mount tends strongly toward the poetic, and the King James translators did not try to dampen down that poetic quality. Jesus' bold metaphor about a body full of light is an example (Matt. 6:22–23): "The light of the body is the eye. If therefore thine eye be single, thy whole body shall be full of light. But if thine eye be evil, thy whole body shall be full of darkness. If therefore the light that is in thee be darkness, how great is that darkness?" I can imagine a reader thinking at this point, What is so special about the King James translators retaining the poetry of the Bible? My answer is that if one surveys how dynamic equivalent translations render Matthew 6:22–23, it is obvious that a poetic Bible is far from the norm in modern translations.

Knowing that poetry does not sound like everyday prose discourse, the King James translators did not experience the anxiety attacks about poetry that afflict modern translators. If the original text says regarding Nabal that "his heart died within him" (1 Sam. 25:37), that is what the King James translators were intent on saying. If Ephesians 5:2 commands believers to "walk in love," that is what the KJV delivers. The King James translators did not even choke on Peter's metaphor "gird up the loins of your mind" (1 Pet. 1:13).

Poetic Rhythm

The King James Bible is as superior in poetic rhythm as it is in prose rhythm. Yet a great lapse needs to be noted in this regard: it was criminal of the King James translators to print poetry as prose. The poetry of the Bible is couched in the verse form of parallelism—two-line units in which the second line repeats all or part of the first line in different words and images. For parallelism to appear to best effect, obviously it needs to be printed as poetry. All that I can say in defense of the King James translators on this score is that it did not occur to any of their predecessors, either, to print the poetry of the Bible in poetic lines rather than prose, and additionally in the original manuscripts poetry was not written in a form that showed the verse construction.

With that critique in place, the claim is still uncontested that the poetry of the King James Bible is rhythmically the best among English translations. All that I said about cadence and smoothness of flow in the preceding chapter applies equally to the poetry of the KJV. As I cite examples, we can see not only the musical genius of the translators, but also the benefits of their having an inflected language with unaccented verb endings to keep the rhythm flowing smoothly.

I will begin by noting how a sampling of commentators on the King James Bible make the case for its rhythmic superiority. Here is Charles Butterworth on the subject:

> The translators were men of sensitive ear. The cadence of their sentences is often unsurpassed. Take for example their rendering of the Psalmist's well-known dictum on the brevity of human life (Psalm 90:10): 'The dayes of our yeres are threescore yeeres and

ten, and if by reason of strength they be fourscore yeeres, yet is their strength labour and sorrow: for it is soone cut off, and we flie away.' This sentence [is noteworthy for] its sustained rhythm and its falling close.[2]

G. S. Paine quotes the King James rendition of Isaiah 9:6 ("For unto us a child is born. . . ."), and then comments, "As we read that, we can hear the music of Handel's *Messiah*. It is splendid verse in groups of balanced words. . . . The rhythms of the King James version are such that, whether or not the verses are set to music, most people seem to recognize that they are poetry."[3]

> "What I call the 'auditory imagination' is the feeling for syllable and rhythm, penetrating far below the conscious levels of thought and feeling, invigorating every word; sinking to the most primitive and forgotten." —T. S. Eliot, *The Use of Poetry and the Use of Criticism*

Lane Cooper, in a monograph entitled *Certain Rhythms in the English Bible*, shows how certain passages of poetry in the KJV fall into the ordinary categories of rhythm found in English poetry. Thus the second verse of Psalm 73 falls into regular iambic feet (consisting of an unaccented syllable followed by an accented syllable): "But AS for ME, my FEET were ALmost GONE; my STEPS had WELL nigh SLIPPED." Verses 3 and 6 of Psalm 23 are predominantly anapestic (two unaccented syllables followed by an accented one, to make a poetic foot consisting of three syllables): "he reSTOReth my SOUL"; "I [unaccented] will DWELL in the HOUSE of the LORD for EVer."

Good poetic rhythm came naturally to the King James translators because they lived in an oral culture in which the Bible was read daily in religious settings. The language they used had the additional rhythmic benefit of unaccented inflected verb endings: "whatsoEVer he DOeth shall PROSper" (Ps. 1:3); "thou VISITest the EARTH and WATerest it" (Ps. 65:9). When modern translators make a conscious break with the King James tradition, the deficiency in rhythm shows itself repeatedly. For a specimen, we can compare the following two versions of Psalm 24:1:

> The EARTH is the LORD'S and the FULness thereOF;
> The WORLD, and THEY that DWELL thereIN.

> The EARTH is the LORD's and ALL that is IN IT,
> the WORLD, and ALL who DWELL IN IT.

I chose this as an example of how some of the archaic constructions of the KJV (in this case the words *thereof* and *therein*) are a great aid to smooth rhythm. Robbed of those resources, the second rendition quoted above ends the lines in a jolting and staccato manner.

I have barely scratched the surface on poetic rhythm in the King James Bible, but it is not a subject that requires extended discussion. The proof will emerge if we simply hear the poetry of the King James Bible with our ears.

Exaltation and Affective Power

Poetry is affective in the sense of expressing and activating feeling, whereas expository prose achieves its effects by rational or intellectual means. As I explore the affective nature of the KJV in this section of the chapter, I will move beyond the poetry of the King James Bible to encompass prose and other genres as well. In doing so, however, I am still in the realm of poetic *effects* in the KJV. I will briefly answer three questions:

1. Does the KJV possess a quality of exaltation?
2. What constitutes the evocative power of the King James Bible?
3. Why is it important that an English Bible convey a sense of the elevated as opposed to the merely prosaic?

Tributes to the exaltation and eloquence of the King James Bible date back a long way. In the first half of the twentieth century we find statements about the "lofty grandeur of the diction of the English Bible," about the "lofty imagination" and "noble style" of the KJV, and about how "the majesty of the rhythm fits the nobility of the thought."[4]

Nonetheless, assertions regarding the affective and imaginative splendor of the King James Bible absolutely exploded when new translations began to appear in the middle of the twentieth century. Most reviewers of the new translations could hardly contain their disparaging comments about the new translations when compared with the grandeur and elegance of the KJV.[5] That is the context of the following statements:

- "To make the Bible readable in the modern sense means to flatten out, tone down and convert into tepid expository prose what in K.J.V. is wild, full of awe, poetic, and passionate. It means stepping down the voltage of K.J.V. so it won't blow any fuses."[6]
- "I find the new text inferior on nearly every page to the one it seeks to supplant. . . . It is weaker, less vivid, defective in imagery, less beautiful, and less inspired."[7]
- "The danger with modernizers is that they can become crude, uncouth. . . . That kind of familiarity, too, can breed contempt. . . . The New English Bible . . . seems to alter [the KJV] wantonly, and for the worse—to exchange dignity, or beauty, for a banal breeziness—to stagger into wordiness, imprecision, or downright untruth."[8]

A cluster of related concepts converge in these defenses of the KJV against the practices of many modern translators. They include eloquence, mystery, evocativeness, exaltation, and an ability to elevate.

Is it possible to explain how the King James Bible produces these qualities and effects? My final answer is that it is not possible fully to explain the King James magic, but that does not mean that we should not analyze some of the techniques and practices

149

of the King James translators. If much remains elusive, we can note big and small techniques that enter the equation.

In the previous chapter I observed the King James formulas *lo, behold,* and *verily* as stylistic touches that elevate the grandeur of an event or statement in the King James Bible. The poetic equivalent is what is called the vocative, represented in the King James Bible by the single letter O: "Teach me, O LORD, the way of thy statutes" (Ps. 119:33). The functions of the vocative O are multiple. Sometimes it initiates a direct address to a person, including God (in which case it functions as part of an invocation): "O LORD, thou hast searched me and known *me*" (Ps. 139:1). Sometimes this direct address is directed to a personification as part of the poetic technique known as apostrophe: "O death, where is thy sting? O grave, where is thy victory?" (1 Cor. 15:55). Sometimes it functions as an exclamation: "O magnify the LORD with me" (Ps. 34:3).

> "In all languages I know of it has been the universal tendency to express the central ideas of religion in a language more dignified, more archaic even, and with more implicit levels of meaning than that used for the doings of ordinary life." —C. L. Wrenn, review of the New English Bible

Some modern translators pride themselves on having liberated their readers from this allegedly archaic formula, but what they have actually done is depleted some of the exaltation that is a hallmark of the King James Bible. The KJV renders Psalm 34:8 this way: "O taste and see that the LORD *is* good." The voltage is lowered in the common modern way of translating the statement: "Taste and see that the LORD is good."

Vocabulary no doubt plays its part in the affective power of the King James Bible, but this is very hard to analyze. Here is a typical King James specimen: "Come unto me all ye that labour and are heavy laden, and I will give you rest" (Matt. 11:28). Enthusiasts for the King James Bible and debunkers of it are likely to use similar descriptors for such a verse: *stately, sonorous, polished, beautiful.* But the vocabulary is actually simple and not inherently elegant. So why does it strike us as so evocative? I speak of a great mystery. We might say that the content of the verse is what makes it moving, not the form. Charles Butterworth thus writes that anyone who reads the verse "sees before him a doorway of release, and no disquisition on the beauty of the words could make them more acceptable."[9] But the same content in a typical modernizing translation is flat and prosaic: "Come to me, all of you who are tired and have heavy loads, and I will give you rest" (NCV). Part of what strikes modern readers as elegance in the King James Bible is its archaic quality (e.g., the construction *heavy laden*), but the diction and syntax in the quoted passage are actually simple.

The prevailing simplicity of language in the King James Bible does not mean that the language is never exalted. The salutations that appear at the beginning of the New Testament Epistles can nearly always be trusted to supply an example of "big words" and complex sentence structure:

> For as the sufferings of Christ abound in us, so our consolation also aboundeth by Christ. And whether we be afflicted, *it is* for your consolation and salvation, which is effectual in the enduring of the same sufferings which we also suffer: or whether we be comforted, *it is* for your consolation and salvation. (2 Cor. 1:5–6)

In this passage, the vocabulary and sentence structure are both lofty.

The syntax of the King James Bible is a frequent source of affective power. On the day when I teach prose styles in seventeenth-century English literature, I stand before my class and announce that I am going to read the very touchstone of embellished prose in English literature. I then ask my students to guess what that passage is. It begins this way:

> Though I speak with the tongues of men and of angels, and have not charity, I am become as sounding brass or a tinkling cymbal. And though I have the gift of prophecy, and understand all mysteries and all knowledge: and though I have all faith, so that

151

I could remove mountains, and have not charity, I am nothing.
(1 Cor. 13:1–2)

This is a rhetorically formal passage, employing repetition, doublets (pairs joined by *and*), and suspended sentence structure (in which we need to keep reading before the sentence is completed).

But even after we name such things as formal constructions, distinctive vocabulary (whether simple or formal), and sophisticated syntax, we have not accounted for what makes the King James Bible uniquely evocative and moving. Something has fallen like a benediction on the King James Bible, but what that "something" is remains elusive. Psalm 34:19 begins as follows in the KJV: "Many are the afflictions of the righteous." Thinking to improve on the vocabulary and inverted sentence structure of the KJV, modern translations show us by their flatness how elevating the KJV is: "a righteous man may have many troubles" (NIV); "the LORD's people may suffer a lot" (CEV); "people who do what is right may have many problems" (NCV).

Why does it matter that an English Bible possess the kind of exaltation that the KJV displays? To begin, an exalted Bible elevates the mind, heart, and soul in a way that a mundane translation does not. "Modern English," writes Henry Seidel Canby, "is lacking in eloquence, in its root sense of speaking out, and its acquired meaning of speaking out from the heart"; this is in contrast to the King James Bible, whose style is "eloquent and almost unequaled in emotional expressiveness," leaving "our religious life . . . quickened and the mind exalted."[10]

"Every morning before breakfast we assembled in the sitting room and my father read a passage from the [King James] Bible, followed by a prayer. . . . Somewhere, as my father read, I became excitedly aware of something more than the story: of the beauty and glory of the words; of the images they can evoke and the thoughts they can enkindle." —Dorothy Thompson, "The Old Bible and the New"

In addition to this argument based on reader response, we can say something about how an exalted style does justice to the content of the Bible in ways that a prosaic translation does not. Dwight Macdonald has stated correctly that "the religious passion of Jesus and Paul . . . needs an exalted idiom to be adequately conveyed." [11] Likewise with the mystery of the supernatural that pervades the Bible: someone has said that "another quality that can fairly be demanded of a Bible is mystery," which evaporates in modern translations. [12]

Another reason the majesty of the KJV matters is that the majesty evokes a sense of authority for the Bible. Adam Nicolson has written well on the subject, as follows: "One of the King James Bible's most consistent driving forces is the idea of majesty. Its method and its voice are . . . regal. . . . Its qualities are those of grace, stateliness, scale, power. There is no desire to please here; only a belief in the enormous and overwhelming divine authority." [13]

A Simplicity That Enlarges

Two words that regularly surface in regard to the KJV are *simplicity* and *majesty*. Sometimes both words appear in catalogs of adjectives describing the KJV. Here are three specimens:

- "There is a kind of monosyllabic simplicity and yet majesty about much of the language." [14]
- "But simplicity is not the only quality of the diction of the King James version. It has majesty and stateliness as well." [15]
- "All these factors combined to produce the clarity, simplicity, passion, beauty and majesty of the King James Bible which has outlasted all subsequent revisions." [16]

How can the King James Bible be both simple and majestic? I propose that this paradox can be resolved if we accept a principle that Clyde S. Kilby once expressed (not in connection with the KJV). "There is a simplicity which diminishes," wrote Kilby, "and a simplicity which enlarges."[17] One of the tricks that modern colloquializing translators try to play on a gullible public is to claim that the simple vocabulary of much of the Bible proves that translations should sound like everyday colloquial speech. But this does not follow at all: the simple can be a form of beauty and elegance as well as the low and common.

Some parts of the King James Bible fall decisively into one of the two categories I have named. The following passage is simplicity personified: "And the servant ran to meet her, and said, Let me (I pray thee) drink a little water of thy pitcher. And she said, Drink, my lord: and she hasted, and let down her pitcher upon her hand, and gave him drink" (Gen. 24:17–18). The King James style is archaic for modern readers, and the event of Abraham's servant meeting Rebekah at the well is momentous, but the narrative style is direct and simple.

> "The simplicity of the AV style has often been praised, and this too is a quality that belongs to the original. But there are different kinds of simplicity. . . . The simplicity of the Bible is the simplicity of majesty, not of equality, much less of naiveté: its simplicity expresses the voice of authority. The purest verbal expression of authority is the word of command."
> —Northrop Frye, *The Great Code of Art*

When the original text is itself couched in a high style, the King James Bible is similarly exalted. The prologue to John's Gospel echoes a famous hymn to Zeus that the ancient Greeks had sung for centuries by the time John wrote it: "In the beginning was the Word, and the Word was with God, and the Word was God. The same was in the beginning with God. All things were made by him, and without him was not anything made that was made" (John 1:1–3). Word patterns and other patterns of repetition make this passage poetic and rhetorically embellished.

Overall, then, we can say that the King James Bible as a whole is both simple and grand. Some passages specialize in simplicity, others in eloquence.

But to say only that would be to omit one of the great mysteries of the King James Bible, which is that more often than not the effect of majesty is actually expressed in simple vocabulary and syntax. Here is an example of the kind of passage that is the norm in the King James Bible: "Ask, and it shall be given you; seek, and ye shall find; knock, and it shall be opened unto you. For everyone that asketh, receiveth; and he that seeketh, findeth; and to him that knocketh, it shall be opened" (Luke 11:9–10). The vocabulary is simple, and the sentence elements are brief. On the other side, the passage is a rhetorical *tour de force* with its elaborate patterns of repetition. It is, in fact, an example of simple form and majestic effect.

Often a quality of spiritual mystery emerges from the "majestic" half of the equation—an intimation of a transcendent reality beyond the earthly that prosaic modern translations simply lack. Hebrews 12:22–24 is a "high style" passage that illustrates perfectly the claim of Greek dramatist Aristophanes that "high thoughts must have high language":

> But ye are come unto Mount Zion, and unto the city of the living God, the heavenly Jerusalem, and to an innumerable company of angels: to the general assembly and church of the first born which are written in heaven, and to God the judge of all, and to the spirits of just men made perfect: and to Jesus, the mediator of the new covenant, and to the blood of sprinkling that speaketh better things than that of Abel.

Aphoristic Quality

Nearly all that we might claim for the literary excellence of the King James Bible converges in its overarching aphoristic quality. An aphorism is a concise, memorable statement. The King James Bible is the most aphoristic book in the English language. David Daniell comments that "the language of KJV is beautiful. Right through the sixty-six books of the Bible . . . phrases of lapidary beauty have been deeply admired."[18] Victorian poet Francis Thompson, writing about "Books that Influenced Me," singled out the aphoristic quality of the Bible as the trait that he found most noteworthy—the Bible "as a treasury of *gnomic* wisdom"—and he further noted that other "sacred books" of the world lack "the same grave dignity of form and richness of significance in their maxims."[19]

> "The diction of the [KJV] has this power of enchantment in a most remarkable degree. The sheer beauty of its phraseology arrests the attention and then lingers in the memory like haunting strains of music." —Charles Dinsmore, *The English Bible as Literature*

What makes a statement memorable and aphoristic? Nearly always it consists of doing something unusual with language. Poetry tends to be more aphoristic than prose, but in the King James Bible aphorisms appear on nearly every page. What I have called the "unusual" element that produces aphoristic effect can be the presence of vivid imagery and metaphor, but often what we call "a well-turned phrase" gains its effect through special qualities of syntax. Aphorisms are often tight and concise statements, and often they invert normal word order. Whatever the technique, aphoristic writing (with poetry the prime exhibit) possesses the quality that J. R. R. Tolkien attributed to fantasy, namely, arresting strangeness.

What are the benefits of writing that possesses an aphoristic flair? Chiefly three: such discourse is (a) beautiful, (b) striking in its impact, and (c) memorable. The King James translators intuitively knew that. Translators of modern prosaic Bibles engage in a self-defeating venture when they produce Bibles that do not yield the effects common to readers of the King James Bible and its heirs. A Bible translation that sounds like the daily newspaper is given the same level of attention and credence as the daily newspaper.

A single comparison will need to suffice as an illustration. The King James rendition of 1 Timothy 6:6 is oracular: "But godliness with contentment is great gain." Here is an aphorism that not only expresses an insight—it compels it. Here is how three modern translations manage to drain the verse of its power: "well, religion does make a person very rich, if he is satisfied with what he has"; "but godliness *actually* is a means of great gain, when accompanied by contentment"; "and of course religion does yield high dividends, but only to those who are content with what they have." Someone has correctly said that modern colloquial translations "slip more smoothly into the modern ear," but they also slide "out more easily; the very strangeness and antique ceremony of the old forms make them linger in the mind."[20]

Summary

The poetry of the King James Bible is one of its greatest triumphs. Because the translators kept close to the original text, their poetic passages possess the vividness and figurative richness that characterize great poetry. Additionally, their poetry displays rhythmic proficiency. The King James Bible also embodies the qualities of simplicity, majesty, exaltation, and mystery to a preeminent degree among English translations.

Further Reading

Charles Allen Dinsmore, *The English Bible as Literature* (1931).
Dennis Nineham, ed., *The New English Bible Reviewed* (1965).
D. G. Kehl, ed., *Literary Style of the Old Bible and the New* (1970).

11

ACCLAIM FOR THE KING
JAMES BIBLE BY THE LITERARY
ESTABLISHMENT

The Bible translation that I use is the one most familiar to English-speaking people, the King James version (KJV) of 1611. This translation . . . has exerted a stronger influence on English language and literature than any other book. It is, indeed, the only English version of the Bible that enjoys any literary influence.

—STEPHEN COX, *The New Testament and Literature*

THIS CHAPTER WILL SERVE as a transition between the foregoing discussion of the literary merits of the King James Bible and the last section of this book, which will explore the King James Bible as an influence on English and American authors. The focus of this chapter is the virtually unanimous preference of the literary establishment for the King James Bible over other English translations.[1]

It will come as no surprise that English and American authors, as well as literary critics, prefer the King James Version. I suspect, though, that the vehemence with which they prefer the KJV will come as a mild shock. The problem that I faced in composing this chapter was avoiding overkill. I have accordingly kept the chapter brief. I will note in passing that I do not remember ever having encountered a member of the literary establishment who preferred any English Bible other than the KJV.

It will quickly become evident that the preference of literary people for the King James Bible is based on style and literary qualities. Another thing to note is that most of my quotations come from twentieth-century authors and critics. Until then, authors and critics spoke simply of "the Bible," by which they meant the King James Bible. Not until the proliferation of translations in the mid-twentieth century did literary people have a reason to single out the KJV when they spoke about the Bible and literature.

Authors' Praise of the King James Bible

The KJV came into its own as a favorite book of English authors during the romantic movement at the beginning of the nineteenth century. English poet William Blake called the King James Bible "astonishing," explaining that the New Testament corresponds "almost word for word" with the Greek, and that "if the Hebrew Bible is as well translated, which I do not doubt it is, we need not doubt of its having been translated as well as written by the Holy Ghost."[2] Samuel Taylor Coleridge, whose annotated copy of the KJV survives, wrote that "the words of the Bible find me at greater depths of my being" than "all other books put together." Elsewhere he asked rhetorically, "Did you ever meet any book that went to your heart so often and so deeply?"[3]

Twentieth-century authors express similar sentiments, but now in a context of preferring the KJV over other translations. William Styron said, "I consider the King James Version to be the *only* worthwhile version for its style and poetry." American author John Dos Passos called the KJV "the fountainhead of good English prose," and he further recalled that "Ernest Hemingway and I, when we first knew each other, both in our early twenties, agreed that there just was no narrative to beat parts of Samuel, Kings, and Chronicles."

Four Verdicts from Literary Authors on the King James Bible

- "Immeasurably superior" to other translations (W. H. Auden).
- "All-supreme" (Eudora Welty).
- "Infinitely superior" to other translations (Wallace Stegner).
- "Unmatchable" (Christopher Fry).

Christopher Fry, after calling the KJV "unmatchable," went on to say that "to those who know it well there must always be a feeling of lack when other words are used. . . . It is a great work of creation as well as translation. Its style is a radical part of what the Bible means to us." Poet John Ciardi offered the opinion, "I hold [the KJV] to be stylistically superior to all other versions. I don't see how anyone drawn to the English language can afford to miss it."

It is not only as readers of the Bible that novelists and poets praise the KJV; they also pay tribute to it as an influence on their writing. American author Howard Nemerov said regarding the King James Bible that "its force remains in much that I try to do in poetry and stories." Fiction writer John Cheever said, "I've been listening to [the KJV] for over forty years and it's bound to have made an impression."

Wallace Stegner claimed that "it is impossible to have had a literary education without being strongly influenced by Biblical cadences and phrasing." Poet and anthology editor Louis Unter-meyer wrote, "The King James Version is the only version I use, and I use it constantly." Beatrix Potter was known to read the Authorized Version when she felt that her prose style needed to be "chastened" (that is, simplified and pared down). Fiction writer Eudora Welty wrote autobiographically, "How many of us, the South's writers-to-be of my generation, were blessed . . . in not having gone deprived of the King James Version of the Bible. Its cadence entered into our ears and our memories for good. The evidence . . . lingers in all our books."[4]

Unlikely Enthusiasts for the King James Bible

While few of the authors and critics quoted in this chapter were people of religious faith, they are not known as antagonists of Christianity. But the enthusiasts for the King James Bible include surprises. Sometimes those who endorse the KJV wish to make sure that their praise is not understood as religiously motivated. Wallace Stegner is an example:

> The King James as a literary document is infinitely superior [to other translations]. . . . It is a work of genius in literary terms; its language has the leap and spark and plasticity of one of the

---

Numerous anthologies have been published containing literary works based on specific parts of the Bible. Sometimes the relevant biblical passage is printed along with the corresponding literary works. This naturally requires the editors to decide which English translation to use. Here are the editors' explanations of their choices from the prefaces of two anthologies:

- *The Enduring Legacy: Biblical Dimensions in Modern Literature*, ed. Douglas C. Brown (1975): "A glance at the list should help to explain why the King James version of the Bible . . . has been used throughout. . . . It is this translation which, for more than three-and-a-half centuries, has been the most familiar to English-speaking writers and readers, and thus is the version that has most directly influenced our language and literature."
- *Chapters into Verse: A Selection of Poetry in English Inspired by the Bible from Genesis through Revelation*, ed. Robert Atwan and Laurance Wieder (2000): "The decision to use the King James Bible was not so much ours as it was the authors we included. So many important poets since the seventeenth century have relied on this Bible's resonant style . . . that it made no literary or editorial sense for us to use any other version or translation. . . . The King James Bible is itself a monumental literary achievement."

---

great ages of languages. For my own purposes, which are not religious, I would never feel the need of having any other Bible in the house.

The notorious nonconformist H. L. Mencken called the King James Bible "unquestionably the most beautiful book in the world," a book with "poems so overwhelmingly voluptuous and disarming that no other literature, old or new, can offer a match for it."[5] And George Bernard Shaw wrote:

> In all these instances [of Bible distribution] the Bible means the translation authorized by King James the First. . . . The translation was extraordinarily well done because to the translators what they were translating was . . . the word of God divinely revealed through His chosen and expressly inspired scribes. In this conviction they carried out their work with boundless reverence and care and achieved a beautifully artistic result.[6]

Literary Scholars and the King James Bible

Beyond literary authors is the guild of literary scholars and teachers. They are just as vocal in their preference for the King James Bible. D. G. Kehl, who edited the most helpful book on the subject of this chapter, offered his own opinion that "rather than gaining clarity, as some would insist, . . . most of the spate of modern versions sacrifice beauty for banality, vigor for vapidity." Kehl also made the summary statement that "the consensus among literary people—poets, fictionists, essayists, critics—is that the Authorized Version or King James Version is superior in literary style to any other version."[7]

David Daiches, esteemed British literary scholar of an earlier era, wrote:

> The question of whether I consider the style of the Authorized Version of the Bible to be better than that of modern versions is hardly one that is open to dispute. Everybody knows that the Authorized Version came at the end of a great period of rich de-

velopment in Tudor biblical prose and that in literary quality . . . it stands unique.

Language expert Mario Pei claimed that his "own taste runs to the King James in preference to modern versions." Joseph Wood Krutch wrote, "In general I have always preferred the King James Version simply because it has what seems to be an appropriate flavor of a past time." Jacques Barzun believed that the KJV has "the advantage of general acceptance and antiquity over later versions." And literary critic Mark Schorer called the King James Bible "the greatest English text."

Robert Penn Warren advised aspiring writers to "read your Bibles and mark them well. And I mean the King James Version." Mary Ellen Chase, in writing for what she called "the common reader" of the Bible, offered her opinion that "if we would truly understand [English and American authors], we must know the Bible in its one translation which they knew and honoured."[8]

Academic Teaching of the Bible as Literature

The "Bible-as-literature" movement is nearly a century old. The "institutional" forms of this movement are (a) a series of anthologies of selections of the Bible intended for use in high school and college literature and courses, (b) a host of academic courses in which the English Bible is taught as literature, and (c) books of literary criticism spawned by those courses. As Reynolds Price correctly observes, the King James Bible is the version that is used "in a thousand college courses on 'The Bible as Literature.'"[9] A survey of Bible-as-literature courses that have an Internet site will quickly confirm this observation.

The era of the 1930s and 1940s saw a flowering of literary introductions and surveys of the English Bible as literature—books with titles like *The Bible as English Literature*, *The English Bible as Literature*, *The Literature of the English Bible*, and *The Bible and the Common Reader*. By modern scholarly standards, these books have a naiveté about them, especially in their virtual equation of "the Bible" (and not simply the English Bible) with the

---

Here are two "quotable quotes" from literary experts that express insight into the uniqueness of the King James Bible:

- Literary scholar Howard Mumford Jones said that the King James Bible "can be parodied but it cannot be paralleled."
- John Steinbeck, who "much preferred the KJV to any other," saw a movie based on the Bible and then quipped, "Saw the movie. Loved the book."

KJV. In making a point about "the Bible," the authors of these books quote from the KJV as though it *were* the Bible.

As for the anthologies that made the Bible-as-literature movement possible, three of the most important are the following, each accompanied by a statement from the editor about the choice of the KJV:

- *The Bible Designed to Be Read as Living Literature*, ed. Ernest Sutherland Bates (1936): The literary purpose of this anthology "dictates the use of the King James translation" except with selected books.
- *The Bible for Students of Literature and Art*, ed. G. B. Harrison (1964): "The translation chosen is the King James version, which for three hundred and fifty years has been the most familiar to English-speaking writers and readers of all kinds."
- *The Bible: Selections from the King James Version for Study as Literature*, ed. Roland M. Frye (1965): "Nor can any more recent translation be said to equal or even approach the literary stature" of the KJV.

Preference for the KJV over Modern Translations

Sometimes we can piece together how authors feel about the King James Bible from negative comments that they make about modern translations. T. S. Eliot is the most famous example. When the New English Bible appeared, Eliot published an extended review in the London *Sunday Telegraph* (December 16, 1962). References to the KJV rise to the surface periodically as Eliot conducts a relentless criticism of what he regarded as infelicitous renditions of the NEB. The basis of the comparison is largely stylistic (with clarity one aspect of style). Compared to the Authorized Version, Eliot asserts, "We ask in alarm, 'What is happening to the English language?'" Since the Elizabethan age "was richer in writers of genius than is our own," writes Eliot, "we should not expect a translation made in our time to be a masterpiece of our literature . . . as was the Authorised Version of 1611." It was in this review that Eliot rendered his famous verdict that modern Bible translations are "an active agent of decadence."

Eliot is not alone. Conrad Aiken wrote, "Of course anyone would prefer the King James version to any of the later improvements, so-called. Frightful!" Allen Tate said that "the modern versions . . . are dull and vulgar." And for Walter Van Tilburg Clark, "None of the revised or modern versions can begin to compare with KJV. What they may gain here and there in accuracy is nothing as compared with what they lose in the power to move."

Summary

The subject of this chapter has been specific and focused—the sentiments of poets, fiction writers, playwrights, and literary essayists regarding the King James Bible. These literati overwhelmingly—perhaps unanimously—regard the KJV as superior to all other English Bible translations.

Further Reading

Robert T. Oliver, "The Bible and Style," *Sewanee Review* 42 (1934): 350–55.

D. G. Kehl, ed., *Literary Style of the Old Bible and the New* (1970).

PART FOUR

The Literary Influence
of the King James Bible

12

LITERATURE AND THE BIBLE

For this purpose [of exploring the Bible as literature] there seemed
no choice but the Authorized Version of 1611. . . . It invites the
response of all great literature: wonder, delight, exaltation. . . . It
achieves as we read a strange authority and power as a work of
literature. It becomes one with the Western tradition, because it
is its single greatest source.

—T. R. HENN, *The Bible as Literature*

BEFORE WE EXPLORE how the King James Bible has influenced
specific English and American authors through the centuries, we
need to get a clear picture of exactly how the Bible can enter a
work of literature. In this chapter I will conduct an anatomy of the
specific ways in which the Bible functions in works of literature
where an author has made it a part of the work.

The Bible as Literary Source, Influence, and Presence

The single most important critical statement about the biblical
presence in literature comes from C. S. Lewis in a famous essay
entitled "The Literary Impact of the Authorised Version."[1] Lewis
begins his discussion by proposing to distinguish "the various

senses in which one book can be said to influence the author of another book." The first way, according to Lewis, is that a work can serve as a source for an author, and having stated that, Lewis almost immediately produces his much-quoted principle: "A Source gives us things to write about; an Influence prompts us to write in a certain way."

This provides a useful lens through which to assess what is happening when we read works of literature that bear an obvious relationship to the Bible. There are many instances where authors begin with a story, character, or situation from the Bible, and then exercise their imagination on it. In fact, for more than half a century now publishers have printed anthologies of such works (usually poems).[2]

Distinctly different from that category of biblically based works are works in which authors begin not with the Bible but with the ordinary process of choosing experiences and story material for presentation. In the process of working out their imaginative vision, writers can then follow the Bible as a model, or allow it to influence them in other ways. The Bible does not give them their subject matter, but it prompts them to elaborate their independently chosen material in certain ways.

The distinction between the Bible as a source and influence is an excellent starting point, but it does not cover the whole territory. This becomes evident when we consider biblical allusions in literature, as in Milton's reference to Jesus' parable of the talents when he speaks of "that one talent which is death to hide" (Milton's sonnet on his blindness). Literary scholars regularly speak of the "source" of an allusion, but regarding Milton's biblical reference in his sonnet on his blindness the Bible certainly does not function as a source in the same way that it is a source for Milton's *Paradise Lost* and *Samson Agonistes*. Nor is it quite on target to speak of the parable of the talents as having influenced Milton's sonnet.

We are on safest ground, therefore, to introduce a broader concept into the picture, that of the biblical *presence* in literature.[3] Whenever the concepts of source and influence appear inadequate, we can simply speak of the presence of the Bible in a work or passage of literature.

In the rest of this chapter, I will provide an anatomy of ways in which the Bible enters imaginative literature. For each point that I make, I will provide a single illustration. The purpose of the illustration is to make sure that the principle is clear. In the three subsequent chapters I will build on the foundation that I lay in this chapter.

How the Bible Functions as a Literary Source and Influence

According to the paradigm that C. S. Lewis bequeathed, the Bible functions as a source when it gives a writer something directly. Here is a brief list of things that writers import directly from the Bible into their works, in effect using the Bible as a source:

- Title of a novel: *The Power and the Glory* (Graham Green)
- Title of a play: *Measure for Measure* (William Shakespeare)
- Title of a poem: "Many Are Called" (Edwin Arlington Robinson)
- Title of a short story: "A Temple of the Holy Ghost" (Flannery O'Connor)
- Epigraph at the beginning of a novel: "Verily, verily, I say unto you, except a corn of wheat fall into the ground and die, it abideth alone: but if it die, it bringeth forth much fruit, John 12:24" (dedication page of *The Brothers Karamazov*, English language editions)
- Epigraph at the beginning of a poem: "And when this epistle is read among you, cause that it be read also in the church of the Laodiceans" (T. S. Eliot, "The Hippopotamus")
- Chapter title in a novel: "The Valley of the Shadow of Death" (Charlotte Bronte, *Shirley*)
- Name of a character in a story: Ishmael and Captain Ahab (Herman Melville, *Moby Dick*)

171

- Place name in a fictional story: Gilead, Iowa (Marilynne Robinson, *Gilead*)

These are localized things that writers take from the Bible as a source. On a more global scale, writers can take a biblical event as the story material for a work. One of the most famous examples in modern times is Archibald MacLeish's play *J. B.* (1958), a dramatic rendering of the Old Testament story of Job. MacLeish's modern-day Job is an American banker-millionaire who loses his family and wealth, just as the Old Testament Job did. MacLeish explained in the foreword to the acting edition of the play that turning to the Bible for a framework seems sensible "when you are dealing with questions too large for you which, nevertheless, will not leave you alone." The theme of the play is humanistic, in obvious contrast to Job's encounter with the transcendent God, but the play stands as an example of a play in which the author took his basic material—a story of exceptional calamity—from the Bible.

> The Bible is "the major informing influence on literary symbolism. . . . Once our view of the Bible comes into proper focus, a great mass of literary symbols from *The Dream of the Rood* to *Little Gidding* begins to take on meaning." —Northrop Frye, *Anatomy of Criticism*

Poets often do the same thing. English romantic poet Lord Byron wrote an amazing poem entitled "The Death of Sennacherib." In a racing anapestic meter (two unaccented syllables followed by an accented syllable), Byron recreates the event narrated in 2 Kings 19:35 and Isaiah 37:36. Here is the opening stanza of the poem:

> The Assyrian came down like the wolf on the fold,
> And his cohorts were gleaming in purple and gold;
> And the sheen of their spears was like stars on the sea,
> When the blue wave rolls nightly on deep Galilee.
> Like the leaves of the forest when Summer is green,

That host with their banners at sunset were seen:
Like the leaves of the forest when Autumn hath blown,
That host on the morrow lay withered and strown.

The poem is of course an imagined embellishment on the brief narrative of the Old Testament chronicle, but it is an example of how a poet starts with something from the Bible as the kernel for his own composition. Without the Bible, a poem like this would not exist.

In the foregoing examples, the Bible provided the initial situation with which the authors worked. In an alternate process, authors start, not with the Bible, but with their own independently conceived literary vision. In working out their composition, they allow the Bible to influence this or that aspect of their form or content.

For example, a story in the Bible can provide the skeleton around which authors build their own story. Thomas Hardy's novel *The Mayor of Casterbridge* is a story set in Hardy's favorite locale—rural England. At the heart of the story is a generational conflict between a middle-aged man and a young man who supplants him. It has become a critical commonplace that as the action unfolds, there are many hints that Hardy is developing his plot with the Old Testament story of King Saul and the youthful David in mind. In the very year that Hardy completed *The Mayor of Casterbridge*, he wrote an entry entitled "evidences of art in Bible narratives" in his diary, and the entry included the statement that whereas plots in modern fiction lack a sense of shapeliness, "in these Bible lives and adventures there is the spherical completeness of perfect art."[4]

We might wonder why a novelist would be interested in biblical story patterns for a realistic story set in a contemporary social milieu. We can find an answer in the reply of novelist Joyce Cary to an interviewer's question of whether he based his characters on real life: "Never, you can't. You may get single hints. But real people are too complex and too disorganized for books. They aren't simple enough. Look at all the great heroes and heroines:

. . . they are essentially characters from fable."[5] In other words, the old story patterns of myth, fable, and the Bible represent a repository of paradigms and motifs that can guide a modern storyteller.

> "The truth remains . . . that the translation of 1611 has entered into our literature as no other version has yet had time or authority to do. Knowing it as many of them knew no other book, the great writers of English for three centuries have made it a requirement for the understanding of their own works, indeed of themselves. . . . [They] have woven its words, its characters, its incidents, its imagery, its style into the very fabric of their own literature." —Mary Ellen Chase, *The Bible and the Common Reader*

The Bible can also serve as a model for genres. When Milton late in life composed the grand epic that he had aspired to write since his college years, he went to the classical tradition for the epic genre itself. But *Paradise Lost* is so different from classical epics that it is customary to call it an anti-epic or counter-epic as well as epic. The Bible was the chief model for Milton's revamping of his classically derived genre. For example, the battles in *Paradise Lost* are not between earthly armies but are spiritual and heavenly battles. His epic hero is Christ. Milton's concept of the hero is not the triumphant warrior but the Christian saint who seeks to please God. It is easy to see that the New Testament book of Revelation was what influenced Milton in his handling of the epic genre that he took from the classical tradition.

Another way in which the Bible can influence a writer is stylistic. English romantic poet William Wordsworth looked about him and was repelled by the acquisitive spirit of his age—a spirit that had deadened people's ability to respond with their hearts to nature. He began a sonnet of personal revolt against the values of his age with these two lines: "The world is too much with us; late and soon, / Getting and spending, we lay waste our powers." Stylistically this could be coming straight from the King James

Bible. The opening image of "the world" is not the way we normally speak. Wordsworth is drawing upon certain powerful connotations of the New Testament Bible where "the world" is a shorthand for the fallen values by which people wrongly live: "Love not the world, neither the things that are in the world" (1 John 2:15); "The cares of this world, and the deceitfulness of riches choke the word, and he becometh unfruitful" (Matt. 13:22); "Be not conformed to this world" (Rom. 12:2). We also immediately note the parallel "and" constructions, in imitation of biblical parallelism, as well as the military image of "lay waste," an echo of Psalm 91:6 ("the destruction that wasteth at noonday").

Biblical Allusions and Echoes

In addition to the Bible as a source and influence for writers, there are times when we are simply aware of the presence of the Bible as we are reading, but not as source or influence. Usually we simply call these "allusions" to the Bible, but it turns out that the subject of literary allusion is very complex. An allusion is a reference to past literature or history. Ordinarily we would reserve the word for instances where we think an author consciously put a biblical reference into the text. But often we do not know whether authorial intention was involved, so the broader term *echo* often seems more appropriate. I offer the following grid as an anatomy of ways in which echoes and allusions operate in literature.

There is first of all a category that literary critics often invoke called "unconscious usage" on the part of the writer. This refers to language or phraseology that is reminiscent of the English Bible but that may have resulted from its being so much a part of common parlance that it entered a work of literature without the author's intending it as a reference to the Bible. For example, when William Wordsworth asserts his faith in the benevolence of the universe, he speaks of his "cheerful faith that all which we behold / Is full of blessings" ("Tintern Abbey," lines 133–34). The vocabulary is reminiscent of the King James Bible, but it is too generalized to be identified as an allusion to a specific passage. Bunyan's *Pilgrim's Progress* is perhaps the most sustained example of biblical echo (in addition to biblical allusions) in English literature, as the opening sentence already illustrates: "As I walked through the wilderness of this world, I lighted on a certain place where was a den, and I laid me down in that place to sleep: and, as I slept, I dreamed a dream."

As we move down the continuum, the next step is the straightforward, simple allusion. By this I mean a statement that requires a knowledge of a biblical text in order to construe the statement. Modern Irish poet William Butler Yeats entitled an apocalyptic poem "The Second Coming." The fact that Yeats used a New Testament commonplace of a second coming in a metaphoric sense of the coming age of terror rather than Christ's return at the end of history does not affect my claim that we need to know certain biblical texts before the title means anything. Perhaps the most explicit biblical reference to a second coming is John 14:3, where Christ promises, "I will come again." But other New Testament passages fill out the picture, such as Peter's reference to "the promise of his coming" (2 Pet. 3:4).

> "As I explored the many ways in which the Bible has entered into our literature, I soon concluded it has made its greatest impact in the form of allusions. . . . The fact that authors dealing with secular materials rely on the Bible to drive home a thematic point or a character trait suggests how indispensable the Bible has become to the formation and understanding of our literature." —Roland Bartel, *Biblical Images in Literature*

Moving further down the continuum, we find the complex allusion. Here a reader needs to go beyond a simple identification of an allusion whose meaning is obvious to analysis of *how* an author intended an allusion to function, or *what meanings* the writer wished to convey. On the very last day of the nineteenth century, Thomas Hardy interred the century by writing a meditative landscape poem entitled "The Darkling Thrush" (with the adjective *darkling* being archaic for "in the dark"). Writing in the familiar hymn meter, the pessimist Hardy in effect penned a hymn of the hopeless in which the speaker in the poem denies hope. But what is the exact nature of the hope that the speaker rejects?

In the midst of a totally depressing winter landscape at twilight, a thrush sings a joyful song. Hardy surrounds the bird's song with words that may hint at a Christian frame of reference—*evensong, joy illimited, carolings*. But the climactic signal comes when the speaker asserts he "could think" that the bird's song arose from "Some blessed Hope." *Some blessed Hope*: surely Hardy intended that phrase to trigger our memory of Titus 2:13, which reads, "Looking for that blessed hope, and the glorious appearing of the great God, and our Saviour Jesus Christ." Here is an instance where readers need to move beyond simply identifying a biblical allusion to determining its meaning in the passage where it appears. In Hardy's poem, we come to understand that it is specifically the Christian hope in the life to come that Hardy rejects.

At the far end of the continuum we have references to the Bible that fall into the category that might be labeled "he who has ears to hear, let him hear." I refer to a biblical presence in a work of literature that adds depth of field or added richness to a passage, but only if a reader sees the connection to the Bible. Pip, the youthful protagonist of Charles Dickens's novel *Great Expectations*, manages to escape from a confined life in his hometown village and live a life of self-indulgent and ignominious ease in London based on the generosity of an anonymous benefactor. Pip rises morally when he loses his fortune. Near the end of the story, when he returns to his hometown village, Pip records: "I felt like one who was toiling home barefoot from distant travel, and whose wanderings had lasted many years." The reader who makes no biblical connection can construe the action, but a reader who catches the allusion to the parable of the prodigal son sees a great deal more.

The Role of Readers

It is not only authors who factor into the biblical presence in literature. Readers are also part of the equation. To begin, references to the Bible are no more than a *potential* meaning that authors put into their works. Unless a reader makes the identification and engages in analysis of the relevance of the reference, no biblical presence emerges. To return to Dickens's *Great Expectations*, after Pip loses his wealth and faces the need to build his life anew without his great expectations, he records, "I sold all that I had." Unless a reader connects that with Jesus' reply to the rich young ruler ("Sell all that thou hast"—Luke 18:22), the spiritual significance of what is happening within Pip never emerges.

But there is a more subtle aspect as well. Many literary allusions to the Bible are sufficiently generalized that by themselves they do not tell us whether the author's imagination was formed by the King James Bible or another translation. At a certain point the King James presence might depend on what translation a literary critic brings into the discussion. Returning to *Great Expectations* one more time, after Pip has remained loyal to his benefactor, a man with a criminal past, through the latter's imprisonment and death, Pip records, "I thought of the two men who went up into the Temple to pray," in obvious reference to Jesus' parable of the Pharisee and publican (Luke 18:10–14). By itself, there is no necessary connection with the King James Bible. But when an editor (e.g., the editor of the Penguin edition) adds an endnote in which he quotes the parable from the King James Version, the KJV has in that very moment become a literary presence in *Great Expectations*.

Summary

The King James Bible was a continuous presence in English and American literature from the middle of the seventeenth century to the present day. The ways in which that presence is exerted range from direct source to indirect influence, and then to allusions. In all of these instances, it requires a biblically literate reader to bring the biblical presence to life.

Further Reading

Roland Bartel, ed., *Biblical Images in Literature* (1975).

David Lyle Jeffrey, ed., *A Dictionary of Biblical Tradition in English Literature* (1992).

Leland Ryken, "The Literary Influence of the Bible," in *A Complete Literary Guide to the Bible*, ed. Leland Ryken and Tremper Longman III (1993), 473–88.

13

EARLY LITERARY INFLUENCE
OF THE KING JAMES BIBLE

The Bible is a book-making book. It is literature which provokes literature. . . . The first and most notable fact regarding the influence of the Bible on English literature is the remarkable extent of that influence. It is literally everywhere.

—C. BOYD McAFEE, *The Greatest English Classic*

I HAVE ORGANIZED MY JOURNEY through English and American literature chronologically by eras. Within the successive eras, I have simply selected major authors for discussion. The result is a series of snapshots of the literary influence of the King James Bible. While I have limited my survey to writers whom we know to have used the KJV rather than other English translations, the situation is rendered complex by the fact that some of the authors were people of such intellectual adeptness that they would have read the Bible in its original languages as well as reading the King James Version. In turn, though, they themselves wrote in English, so they could scarcely have failed to be influenced by the KJV while composing even when they read the Bible in Hebrew and Greek.

John Milton

I will begin the story with the most towering figure in my entire survey and the author who is my own scholarly specialty. John Milton (1608–1674) is so thoroughly a Puritan, and the Geneva Bible was so obviously "the Puritan Bible," that I was initially skeptical of the claim in William Riley Parker's definitive biography of Milton that Milton's "own copy of the Bible was a 1612 edition" of the KJV, "perhaps given him by his parents on his fourth birthday."[1] Parker immediately adds that "its diction, its imagery, its rhythms, early became a part of him." Despite the unlikelihood that a brand-new translation given to a preschool child could have become Milton's preferred English translation, the scholarly consensus confirms that this was the case.[2]

In Milton's prose and poetry we can see the whole gamut of ways in which the King James Bible can enter a writer's works. For starters, Milton went to the Bible for the source of his story material in his three major poetic works, as well as his first important lyric poem. In *Paradise Lost*, Milton takes the main story line from the first three chapters of Genesis— the story of God's creation of the world, Adam and Eve's life of innocence in Paradise, and the fall of humankind prompted by the temptation of Satan. Of course in writing a full-scale epic Milton gathered material from many other parts of the Bible as well.

Paradise Regained was Milton's excursion into what he and his contemporaries called a "brief epic." The main plot, again greatly elaborated with material from many parts of the Bible, is the story of Jesus' temptation in the wilderness as recounted in the Gospels of Matthew and Luke. And Milton's "closet drama" *Samson Agonistes* is based on the story of Samson found in Judges 13–16. To these major works we can add a poem that Milton composed during Christmas vacation while a college student—an ode entitled "On the Morning of Christ's Nativity," for which the birth narratives from Matthew and Luke serve as the skeleton that Milton fleshes out.

But that is only the tip of the iceberg regarding the biblical presence in Milton's poetry. Milton's imagination was so saturated with the Bible that it is woven into the very texture of his poems. To choose an example of something that occurs hundreds of times in Milton's long works, Milton in book 3 of *Paradise Lost* composed a dialogue in heaven between the Father and the Son, in imitation of the classical epic convention of an assembly of gods. In pleading on behalf of fallen humanity, the Son urges the Father not to allow humanity to be forever lost. The plea is partly expressed by these words (lines 153–55):

> That be from thee far,
> That far be from thee, Father, who art judge
> Of all things made, and judgest only right.

What is ringing in Milton's ears at that point, and what rings in our ears if we know the King James Bible, are Abraham's words to God when he intercedes for his nephew Lot and "the righteous" of Sodom: "That be far from thee, to do after this manner, . . . that be far from thee: Shall not the Judge of all the earth do right?" (Gen. 18:25).

"A careful study of Milton's use of the Bible in his epic poems reveals the artist's great mind acting as a prism through which the light of the Bible passes to be broken up into all the colors of the rainbow. . . . The fact that neither Milton nor the Authorized Version of the English Bible . . . has ever been successfully equaled or supplanted by imitators or rivals seems peculiarly appropriate." —James H. Sims, *The Bible in Milton's Epics*

Milton's short poems yield equally good illustrations of how (in the words of William Riley Parker) the diction, imagery, and rhythm of the English Bible "became part" of Milton. On the occasion of Milton's becoming totally blind in his early forties, Milton wrote this famous sonnet:

> When I consider how my light is spent
> Ere half my days in this dark world and wide,
> And that one talent which is death to hide
> Lodged with me useless, though my soul more bent
> To serve therewith my Maker, and present
> My true account, lest he returning chide,
> "Doth God exact day-labor, light denied?"
> I fondly ask. But Patience, to prevent
> That murmur, soon replies, "God doth not need
> Either man's work or his own gifts. Who best
> Bear his mild yoke, they serve him best. His state
> Is kingly: thousands at his bidding speed,
> And post o'er land and ocean without rest;
> They also serve who only stand and wait."

Anyone familiar with the King James Bible would say at once that Milton's poem sounds like the KJV. The vocabulary is our first tip-off: most of the words in the poem also appear in the King James Bible, and some of them seem to belong especially to it—*one talent*, *my soul*, *my Maker*, *day-laborer*, *murmur*, *bear his mild yoke*, *stand and wait*. The frame of reference is biblical, chiefly (but not only) in the continuous references to two parables of Jesus—the workers in the vineyard (Matt. 20:1–16) and the talents (Matt. 25:14–30). On a stylistic level, parallel "and" phrases and clauses abound, in imitation of the parallelism of biblical poetry.

George Herbert

George Herbert (1593–1633) is one of the most famous devotional poets of English Christendom. For the last three years of his short life he was an Anglican priest in the English rural parish of Bemerton, adjacent to Salisbury. Anyone as immersed in mainstream Anglicanism as Herbert was in the early seventeenth century was certain to have used the Book of Common Prayer for the Psalms (Coverdale via the Great Bible), but the Authorized Version for the rest of the Bible. This is the conclusion of Chana Bloch in her book *Spelling the Word: George Herbert and the Bible*: "Quotations from the Bible come primarily from the Authorized, or 'King James,' Version . . . , published in 1611, when Herbert was a student at Trinity College. This was the official church Bible throughout his adult life and is obviously the one he would have known best."[3]

One of Herbert's most characteristic techniques comes straight from the format of the Book of Common Prayer and consists of gathering biblical verses from here and there and weaving them into a composition on a given topic. Herbert delineates this very technique of collation in a poem entitled "The Holy Scriptures II." In this poem Herbert claims that in the Bible, "This verse marks that, and both do make a motion / Unto a third, that ten leaves [pages] off doth lie."

The opening quatrain of Herbert's sonnet entitled "Redemption" illustrates the technique. This poem recounts Everyman's conversion, and it begins with the problem that propels the speaker on his quest to find redemption:

> Having been tenant long to a rich Lord,
> Not thriving, I resolved to be bold,
> And make a suit unto him to afford
> A new small-rented [low rent] lease, and cancel the old.

These lines expressing the speaker's discontent with the unregenerate state are a mosaic of separate biblical verses. The epithet *rich Lord* echoes famous verses in the Epistles that speak of "the Lord [who] is rich unto all that call upon him" (Rom. 10:12) and of "God who is rich in mercy" (Eph. 2:4). When the speaker in the poem "resolved to be bold," he became a practitioner of the exhortation in Hebrews 4:16—"let us therefore come boldly unto the throne of grace that we may obtain mercy, and find grace to help in time of need." The play between *old* (the unregenerate state) and *new* (the redeemed soul) draws upon a cluster of

New Testament passages, such as Ephesians 4:22 and 24: "Put off concerning the former conversation, the old man, which is corrupt . . . . And . . . put on that new man, which after God is created in righteousness, and true holiness." By thus bringing together scattered biblical references, Herbert brings resonance and depth of field to his opening scene of a discontented tenant seeking to achieve solvency.

> "There is scarcely a poem in Herbert's *Temple*—one might say scarcely a line—that does not refer us to the Bible. The readers of *The Temple* are assumed to be readers of the Bible as well, a group of initiates with a history and dialect in common. We cannot get past the title page of the volume without some knowledge of Scripture." —Chana Bloch, *Spelling the Word*

A poem entitled "Love, III" also sounds the authentic Herbert note. The poem is structured as a dialogue that has the nature of a back-and-forth debate, and the two characters are the speaker's soul and God's love, presented as a personified host who utters an invitation:

> Love bade me welcome: yet my soul drew back,
>   Guilty of dust and sin.
> But quick-eyed Love, observing me grow slack
>   From my first entrance in,
> Drew nearer to me, sweetly questioning
>   If I lacked anything.
>
> "A guest," I answered, "worthy to be here":
>   Love said, "You shall be he."
> "I, the unkind, ungrateful? Ah my dear,
>   I cannot look on thee."
> Love took my hand, and smiling did reply,
>   "Who made the eyes but I?"
>
> "Truth, Lord; but I have marred them; let my shame
>   Go where it doth deserve."

"And know you not," says Love, "who bore the
    blame?"
    "My dear, then I will serve."
"You must sit down," says Love, "and taste my meat."
    So I did sit and eat.

This divine invitation to an unworthy sinner who reluctantly
accepts the invitation to partake of a meal surely has in view a
sinner's acceptance by God in the moment of conversion, as well
as participation in the sacrament of communion. But the poem
is also a picture of God's welcome of a sinner into heaven. It is
the very last poem in the volume entitled *The Temple*, and it follows poems entitled "Death," "Judgment," and "Heaven." In
fact, a verse from an eschatological discourse of Jesus was almost
certainly the point of departure for Herbert's poem: "Blessed
are those servants, whom the Lord when he cometh, shall find
watching: Verily, I say unto you, that he shall gird himself, and
make them to sit down to meat, and will come forth and serve
them" (Luke 12:37).

I can imagine someone protesting that the biblical presence
in a poem like this would be the same regardless of what English
translation Herbert might have used. But that is an irrelevance.
My interest is not hypothetical reality but actual reality. Once
we know that Herbert's English Bible was the KJV, that is the
Bible we can picture him as reading and incorporating into his
poetry.

John Bunyan

Beginning at the end of the seventeenth century and lasting for two
centuries, the King James Bible and Bunyan's *Pilgrim's Progress*
were the two "best sellers" in evangelical Protestant households.
In the popular imagination, these two books were regarded as
being cut from the same religious and imaginative cloth. The fact
that readers have found these two books a natural pair is more
telling than occasional scholarly attempts, grounded in technical stylistic analysis, to show that Bunyan's style often differs

from the KJV. The Victorian literary giant Thomas Babington Macaulay offered the opinion that Bunyan "knew no language but the English, as it was spoken by the common people. He had studied no great model of composition, with the exception . . . of our noble [KJV] translation of the Bible."[4]

It might be expected that as a Puritan Bunyan (1628–1688) would have used the Geneva Bible, but the evidence points to the King James Bible instead. This is easy to establish from the occasional direct Bible quotations in *The Pilgrim's Progress*. For example, as Christian is engaged in a life-or-death struggle with Apollyon, he reaches for his sword and says, "Rejoice not against me, O mine enemy; when I fall I shall arise." This is verbatim from Micah 7:8 as found in the KJV, but not the Geneva Bible. In this same paragraph that narrates the battle between Christian and Apollyon, we hear Christian asserting, "Nay, in all these things we are more than conquerors through him that loved us." This, too, is verbatim from the King James Bible (Rom. 8:37), but not the Geneva Bible.

> "Read anything of [Bunyan], and you will see that it is almost like reading the Bible itself. He had studied our Authorized Version, which will never be bettered, as I judge, till Christ shall come; he had read it till his whole being was saturated with Scripture. . . . Prick him anywhere; and . . . the very essence of the Bible flows from him. He cannot speak without quoting a text, for his soul is full of the Word of God." —Charles Spurgeon, *Autobiography*

Once we know what translation Bunyan used, we can quickly assess how much he owed to the King James Bible. Through the centuries, and continuing through modern scholarly editions, it has been customary to print *The Pilgrim's Progress* with marginal notes that identify the biblical source or allusion for a given passage.[5] A glance at such an edition confirms historian John Green's famous verdict that "so completely has the Bible become Bunyan's life that one feels its phrases as the natural expression of his thoughts. He has lived in the Bible till its words have become his own."[6]

What all did Bunyan owe to his King James Bible when he came to compose his masterpiece, which he started to write while imprisoned for nonconformist preaching? Bunyan owes his master image and superstructure—a pilgrimage from this world to the heavenly city—to Hebrews 11:13 and 16: "These all died in faith, . . . and confessed that they were strangers and pilgrims on the earth. . . . They desire a better country, that is, a heavenly . . . city." Second, in telling the story of every Christian, Bunyan based many of his narrative events on scenes from the Bible—an opening flight from a City of Destruction (modeled on the destruction of Sodom and Gomorrah), or Christian's losing his burden of sin at the cross. And as already noted, Bunyan wrote in a biblical idiom as if it were his native language. He himself called this idiom "the language of Canaan."

The final verdict on Bunyan's indebtedness to the King James Bible can be given to David Norton, who writes:

> *The Pilgrim's Progress*, more commonly read by generations than any book but the KJB, helped to form a love for the language of the KJB itself. . . . It is difficult to believe that Bunyan did not contribute to a literary as well as a religious sense of the KJB, and that he did not help show later writers ways they might use it.[7]

The Enlightenment

When the English monarchy was restored in 1660, the Christian fervor of English writers like Milton, Herbert, and Bunyan gave way to the spirit of neoclassicism. The King James Bible did not cease to be a literary presence, however. The difference is that the biblical material was used in a largely literary rather than spiritual way, and the Christianity of the author was sometimes nominal. A scholar named E. M. W. Tillyard notes the shift in John Dryden (1631–1700), who partly overlapped with Milton and Bunyan while belonging to the new culture. Regarding the biblical material in Dryden, Tillyard writes that "it looks as if the old material were there; and yet the emphasis has altered, being now on man and off the rest of creation in a new way."[8]

My concern, of course, is not with religious conviction but with the King James Bible as a literary presence. Whenever we find the Bible in Dryden's poetry and drama, as we often do, it is the KJV that is present. An expert on the subject writes, "Dryden lived in a world interpreted by Scripture. For Dryden, 'Scripture' meant the Authorized Version of 1611, the King James Bible, of whose style and . . . accuracy English men and women were proud."[9]

One of Dryden's greatest poems is an exalted eulogy written on the occasion of a woman's death. It is entitled "Ode on the Death of Mrs. Anne Killigrew," and the last stanza begins with a spirited picture of the Last Day of Christian eschatology:

> When in mid-air the golden trump shall sound,
>   To raise the nations under ground;
>   When in the Valley of Jehosaphat
> The Judging God shall close the book of fate,
>   And there the last assizes keep
>   For those who wake and those who sleep;
>   When rattling bones together fly
> From the four corners of the sky . . .

Virtually every line recalls at least one famous verse from the Bible. If we wish to look up the verses that Dryden had in mind as he wrote, it is the King James Bible that we should consult.

As is true of Dryden, Alexander Pope (1688–1744) shows the continuing influence of the King James Bible in the writing of a Catholic author. As a Catholic, Pope can be assumed to have regularly used the Douay Bible, but it turns out that in his poetry Pope shuttled back and forth between the Douay and King James Bible, choosing whichever suited his poetic purpose best.[10] Pope's most famous poem is *The Rape of the Lock*, a satire occasioned by the snipping off of a lock of hair from an aristocratic young woman. As the young heroine worships herself while conducting "the sacred rites of pride" (i.e., primping for the party at Hampton Court that forms the central action of the poem), she is said to adore her image in the mirror "with head uncovered," echoing Paul's comments about improper worship in 1 Corinthians 11:5 (KJV). Later in the story the scissors with which the lock of hair was cut is called "a two-edged weapon," in echo of the "two edged sword" of Hebrews 4:12 (KJV). In the most famous line of the poem, Pope criticizes the trivializing of the Christian faith in the feminine high society that he portrays in the poem. Pope pictures the messy dresser top of the poem's heroine with the line, "Puffs, powders, patches, Bibles, billet-doux." Pope is protesting a world in which the Bible is placed on a par with puffs and powders. What Bible might we picture on Belinda's dresser? The King James Bible had by Pope's time become the standard English Bible.

> The eighteenth century in England witnessed a range of scholarly and literary attempts to replace the KJV. The final result of "the Enlightenment Bible" movement was to leave the KJV in a more entrenched position than ever: "By 1800 the English were looking for familiarity, not strangeness. In particular, they sought a familiar Bible." Attempts to supplant the KJV "failed decisively in the face of the general English affection . . . for the King James Version." —Jonathan Sheehan, *The Enlightenment Bible*

The same prominence of the KJV is discernible in the other two leading neoclassical writers, Jonathan Swift and Samuel Johnson. As an Anglican cleric, Swift (1667–1745) can be assumed to have used the King James Bible. This is so axiomatic to the author of the book *Swift's Use of the Bible* that he quotes from the KJV throughout his book without ever identifying what English translation he means by "the Bible."[11] Swift's most famous literary work is *Gulliver's Travels*, and regarding it the author of the book on Swift's use of the Bible claims that "Swift has used no Biblical quotations or allusions in *Gulliver's Travels*."[12] Of course the Bible can be an influence apart from direct allusions to it, and we should note that the quality of simplicity that

Swift praised in the KJV is also a characteristic of the style of *Gulliver's Travels.*

Swift's most important comments on the King James Bible come in an essay that discusses the need to preserve the high level of English language that was in danger of ebbing out of usage. Swift's two touchstones of excellence in the English language are the King James Bible and the Book of Common Prayer. Swift praises the simplicity of the KJV, and he calls the King James translators "masters of an *English* style much fitter" for translating the Bible into English than found elsewhere.[13]

Samuel Johnson (1709–1784) was a thoroughgoing neoclassicist who was also a committed Christian. He frequently cited the King James Bible in his famous *Dictionary*.[14] He knew the KJV well, but he was so scholarly that his contact with the Bible was as often to the text in its original languages as it was to an English translation. In the preface to his *Dictionary* Johnson claimed that the KJV and the prose of Anglican apologist Richard Hooker were sufficient as models for the language of theology. We can see this in Johnson's religious writings. Here, for example, is an excerpt from a prayer that appears in Johnson's *Prayers and Meditations*:

> Almighty God, heavenly Father, whose mercy is over all thy works, look with pity on my miseries and sins. Suffer me to commemorate, in thy presence, my redemption by thy son Jesus Christ. . . . Take not from me thy Holy Spirit, but incite in me such good desires, as may produce diligent endeavours after thy glory and my own salvation; and when . . . Thou shalt call me hence, receive me to eternal happiness, for the sake of Jesus Christ our Lord. Amen.

Does this sound like the King James Bible? I propose that it does.

Summary

The seventeenth century was the century of greatest biblical influence in English literary history. No subsequent major writers were to show as much indebtedness to the King James Bible as Milton, Herbert, and Bunyan. In the next century, a pattern was established that would be important right to the present moment: writers of less fervent Christian belief (and eventually of no Christian belief) continued to incorporate the King James Bible into their poems and stories.

Further Reading

James H. Sims, *The Bible in Milton's Epics* (1962).

Barbara K. Lewalski, *Protestant Poetics and the Seventeenth-Century Religious Lyric* (1979).

Chana Bloch, *Spelling the Word: George Herbert and the Bible* (1985).

Rebecca Lemon et al., eds., *The Blackwell Companion to the Bible in English Literature* (2009).

14

THE NINETEENTH CENTURY

While biblical allusion had long been a source of religious enrich-
ment in literature, until [the nineteenth century there had] been
only a few instances of the language of the KJB being used for
[purely] literary effect. . . . Such a situation was bound to change
in a time when the KJB was coming to be loved and respected as
English.

—DAVID NORTON, *A History of the Bible as Literature*

THE DOMINANT LITERARY AND CULTURAL movement of
the nineteenth century in England and America was known as
romanticism. It replaced the neoclassic elevation of reason with
an exaltation of feeling. Romantic writers, moreover, gave such
prominence to the individual's imagination that it had the effect
of replacing Christian faith as the prime religious faculty. In England, the Victorian period succeeded romanticism in the second
half of the century.

Even though romantic writers were not orthodox Christians
in belief, we need to keep two things in mind as we explore the
continuing presence of the KJV in the English-speaking world.
First, though the romantic writers generally ceased to be orthodox

Christians, they absolutely loved the Bible and read it incessantly. Second, while the romantic writers were fringe figures within their own societies, the broad cross section of the English and American populations was overwhelmingly Christian, churchgoing, and Bible reading, and as such even more committed to the King James Bible than the leading authors were. As the nineteenth century ran its course, veneration of the Authorized Version became so intense that modern scholar David Norton coined the word "AVolatry" to describe it.[1] In telling the story of the KJV in the nineteenth century, I will continue the format of the previous chapter—a selection of specimen authors and works.

William Blake

The romantic view of the Bible first emerges in the life and writings of William Blake (1757–1827), whose career as a poet, painter, and engraver shows the influence of the Bible at every turn. An early biographer claimed that Blake's "greatest pleasure was derived from the Bible—a work ever in his hand," while a contemporary of Blake called him "a most fervent admirer of the Bible."[2] A document entitled the *Blake Records* reveals that the Bible was the most thumbed from use of his English books.[3] As already noted in an earlier survey of Blake the engraver, we know that the English Bible used by Blake was the KJV.

If we ask how Blake viewed the Bible, the answer is that for him the Bible was preeminently a work of literature, not a religious authority. He famously termed it "the great code of art," the prototype and model for literary imagination. The author of a book entitled *The Biblical Presence in Shakespeare, Milton and Blake* writes that "the Bible is everywhere in Blake's writing, and yet it would seem to have no independent [religious] authority."[4]

Perhaps Blake's most famous poem is a four-stanza lyric that has the status of a folk hymn in England, where it is popularly known as "Jerusalem." (The movie *Chariots of Fire* begins with congregational singing of this hymn at a memorial service.) The

It is no wonder that the King James Bible won the allegiance of the romantic age: it possesses the literary qualities that romanticists particularly prized. Those qualities were primitivism (a preference for the ancient over the contemporary), elemental simplicity, imaginative and affective power, and sublimity. Here are selected comments by romantic writers that praise the King James Bible for these qualities:

- The writings of classical writers cannot compare "against the sublime of the Bible." —William Blake
- "Did you ever meet any book [besides the Bible] that went to your heart so often and so deeply?" —Samuel T. Coleridge
- "The true model of simplicity of style." —Attributed to both William Wordsworth and Samuel T. Coleridge, as reported by a friend
- "Models of sublimity and pathos ['that which arouses emotions']." —Percy B. Shelley, commenting on the books of Job and Song of Solomon
- "The gravity, simplicity and dignity of the language." —Lord Byron, in his praise of the story of King Saul's visit to the Witch of Endor
- "There is in all these parts of the Scripture . . . an originality, a vastness of conception, a depth and tenderness of feeling, a touching simplicity." —William Hazlitt

magical opening lines are, "And did those feet in ancient time / Walk upon England's mountains green?" Already we can sense a biblical subtext: "How beautiful upon the mountains are the feet of him that bringeth good tidings . . ." (Isa. 52:7). The poem continues, "And was the holy Lamb of God / On England's pleasant pastures seen?" The "Holy Lamb of God" that is "seen": in the background lurks John the Baptist's declamation, "Behold the Lamb of God" (John 1:29, 36). The next two lines of the poem ask, "And did the Countenance Divine / Shine forth upon our clouded hills?" A divine countenance that shines forth: Blake is echoing the Aaronic benediction in Numbers 6:25–26: "The LORD make his face shine upon thee . . . : The LORD lift up his countenance upon thee." And this is only the first six lines of the poem!

Another *tour de force* of biblical presence is Blake's poem "The Tyger." What the tiger symbolizes is a perennial scholarly debate that we do not need to resolve in order to catch the biblical format of the poem. The terrifying power of Blake's tiger represents what his age reveled in as an example of the sublime. The format of the poem is a series of questions about the origin of the tiger as a force of nature, as in the opening stanza:

Tiger, tiger, burning bright,
In the forests of the night,
What immortal hand or eye
Could frame thy fearful symmetry?

The model for this format of a series of questions about nature is the catalog of questions that the voice from the whirlwind asks Job about the mysteries of nature (Job 38–41).

William Wordsworth

Like all the English romantic poets, William Wordsworth (1770–1850) would have been continually exposed to the Anglican Prayer Book and Bible at church and school in his youth. In the case of Wordsworth, church attendance continued throughout his adult life as well. Wordsworth even called the Bible "the most interesting and instructive book . . . ever written."[5] Being more romanticist than Christian, Wordsworth did not borrow subject matter or ideas directly from the Bible. The influence was instead stylistic, including vocabulary, syntax, and rhythm.

The biblical presence in Wordsworth ranges from overt allusion to submerged influence. The former is well illustrated in a sonnet that was occasioned by a seaside evening walk by Wordsworth and his young daughter Caroline. The opening line identifies the scene: "It is a beauteous evening, calm and free," and the beginning of the next line adds to the biblical aura by calling the occasion a "holy time." Having set the scene, Wordsworth introduces deity into it in language and imagery that could come straight from the Psalms or the book of Job:

During his sixty-year career as a writer of poetry, Wordsworth composed as many different kinds of poems as it is possible for one poet to write. Among his unlikely ventures was telling the history of the Christian church in England in a sonnet sequence of 132 sonnets. One of them is entitled "Translation of the Bible," and the chief nuggets from a somewhat obscure poem are the following: before the Reformation "the sacred Book" was wrapped "in dusty sequestration"; when it was translated into "our native tongue," "he who guides the plough, or wields the crook" could read and hear it "with understanding spirit"; the English Bible is a "transcendent boon"—the "noblest that earthly King ever bestowed to equalize and bless." These references are a shorthand summary of many events in the history and assessment of English Bible translation.

> Listen! The mighty Being is awake,
> And doth with his eternal motion make
> A sound like thunder—everlastingly.

Those lines represent the response of the adult speaker (Wordsworth). As the poem concludes, Wordsworth asserts the superiority of the child's intuitive and continuous response to nature, and he does so with biblical images of glory:

> Thou liest in Abraham's bosom all the year,
> And worshp'st at the Temple's inner shrine,
> God being with thee when we know it not.

The presence of the King James Bible in such a poem is partly a matter of conscious allusion and partly a style that Wordsworth absorbed by Bible reading and church attendance.

Wordsworth was given to the writing of long autobiographical poems that included explanations of his philosophy of life. Some of these poems were never finished in the form in which Wordsworth originally envisioned them. But Wordsworth was great at writing prologues in which he conceptualizes for us what he hoped to write. One of these famous passages is a "prospectus" for a poem that is variously known as *The Recluse* and *The Excursion*. In a hundred lines, the King James–sounding phrases tumble out: *dear remembrances, our mortal state, blessed consolations in distress, the law supreme, dwell in highest heaven, the heaven of heavens, the choir of shouting angels, pitches her tents, this goodly universe.* It is no wonder that a literary critic claimed that "the entire Prospectus . . . is suffused with the language of the King James Bible."[6]

Probably Wordsworth's best-known poem today is his nature poem familiarly known as "Tintern Abbey." The King James Bible is present in this poem almost continuously, not by way of direct allusions, but as a stylistic influence on language and rhythm. Almost every passage sounds like the KJV. One of the things that Wordsworth does in the poem is provide his view of the stages of human development, defined in terms of changing responses to nature. Although the adult Wordsworth has lost his youthful exuberance for nature, he finds compensating features in his mature experience. Here is how Wordsworth expresses the matter:

> Not for this
> Faint I, nor mourn nor murmur; other gifts
> Have followed; for such loss, I would believe,
> Abundant recompense.

Later in the poem Wordsworth writes,

> this prayer I make,
> Knowing that Nature never did betray
> The heart that loved her; 'tis her privilege
> Through all the years of this our life, to lead
> From joy to joy.

For all the lines and phrases that I have quoted from the poetry of Wordsworth, it would be easy to sit with a concordance of the KJV and quickly find biblical sources and parallels.

Samuel Taylor Coleridge

Wordsworth's friend and sometime collaborator Samuel Taylor Coleridge (1772–1834) eventually became the most thoroughly

Christian of the major English romantic poets. In fact, in his later years he became an influential apologist for high-church Anglicanism, and he wrote at length on the nature and authority of the Bible. My interest is in Coleridge's use of the King James Bible in his poetry, and I can get right to the heart of the matter by noting that during the last decade of his life Coleridge had two books next to his bed—Martin Luther's *Table Talk* and the King James Version of the Bible.[7] Two copies of the KJV belonging to Coleridge have survived, one of them containing numerous notes from Coleridge.[8] David Norton describes Coleridge as having "been closely and lovingly familiar with [the KJV] from earliest childhood" and having "studied it all his life."[9]

In his statements about the Bible, Coleridge showed his allegiance to his romantic age by looking to the KJV as a model of both simplicity and elevation in English style. On the one hand, he believed that "intense study of the Bible will keep any writer from being vulgar in style."[10] In a similar vein, Coleridge attributed "a tone of dignity" and "beautiful forms of language" to the King James Bible and the Anglican liturgy.[11] But for Coleridge the language of the King James Bible was also a model of clarity and simplicity, as well as dignity and eloquence: "Our version of the Bible [is] most valuable in having preserved a purity of meaning," without which the impulse would have been to "refine away the language to mere abstractions."[12]

If the influence of the KJV on Wordsworth was stylistic, the Bible left its imprint on Coleridge's poetry at the broader level of underlying patterns and archetypes. Coleridge's most famous poem, *Rime of the Ancient Mariner*, is the best illustration. To begin, the underlying story line of the poem comes straight from early Genesis. The story of the ancient mariner who shot an albatross is the story of the fall from innocence embodied in a story of Gothic fantasy. Like Adam and Eve's eating the forbidden apple, the killing of the albatross is a perverse act without motive. It results in the cosmic fall of nature, with only the mariner surviving an ensuing apocalyptic devastation.

Although the mariner is converted and forgiven of his appalling mistake, the restoration is only partially complete in this life. It is easy to see how the whole story enacts the biblical view of history. As an overlay on this biblical story line we find the story of Cain (Gen. 4:1–16), who, as the mariner, too, becomes a guilt-haunted wanderer.

> In the Bible "I have found words for my inmost thoughts, songs for my joy, utterances for my hidden griefs, and pleadings for my shame and my feebleness." —S. T. Coleridge, *Confessions of an Enquiring Spirit*
>
> "Are not other books . . . wonderfully efficacious in proportion as they resemble the New Testament?" —S. T. Coleridge, *Notebooks*

But we can sense the KJV at our elbow in the specifics of Coleridge's story as well. The conversion of the mariner is recounted in a single verse in the very middle of the poem, immediately after the mariner has blessed the water snakes in his heart (lines 288–91):

> The self-same moment I could pray;
> And from my neck so free
> The Albatross fell off, and sank
> Like lead into the sea.

As the mariner loses his guilt in the moment of regeneration, we find ourselves situated in the world of Acts with its conversion stories and the New Testament Epistles with their theological explanations of sin being canceled. The detail of the albatross sinking like lead into the sea evokes two famous Old Testament passages: Pharaoh's host "sank as lead in the mighty waters" of the Red Sea (Ex. 15:10), and Micah describes God as casting "all their sins into the depths of the Sea" (Mic. 7:19).

To cite another famous stanza from the poem, the mariner's final vision of the good life is a picture of ordinary Sunday worship in an English parish (lines 601–4):

O sweeter than the marriage feast,
'Tis sweeter far to me,
To walk together to the kirk
With a goodly company!

The King James phrases just flow into our minds as we read: "sweeter also than honey" (Ps. 19:10); "the marriage supper of the Lamb" (Rev. 19:9); "we . . . walked unto the house of God in company" (Ps. 55:14); "goodly" (a stock positive adjective throughout the KJV); and overshadowing the whole stanza, "I was glad when they said unto me: Let us go into the house of the LORD" (Ps. 122:1).

Nathaniel Hawthorne

The best index to the indebtedness of American fiction writer Nathaniel Hawthorne (1804–1864) to the King James Bible comes from James T. Fields, the editor and publisher to whom Hawthorne attributed his success as a writer. Fields claimed that "Hawthorne was a diligent reader of the Bible, and when sometimes, in my ignorant way, I would question in a proof-sheet, his use of a word, he would almost always refer me to the Bible as his authority."[13] The Bible that Hawthorne knew so well was the KJV, and we can see its influence in Hawthorne's most famous work, *The Scarlet Letter*.[14]

Hawthorne's publisher claimed that the author appealed to biblical precedent when questioned about specific words, so we might well start at the lexical level. The archaic vocabulary of *The Scarlet Letter* belongs not to Hawthorne's own day but to the King James Bible. Here is a specimen, from a speech by Rev. Dimmesdale to his tormenter and physician Roger Chillingworth:

"No!—not to thee!—not to an earthly physician!" cried Mr. Dimmesdale, passionately, and turning his eyes, full and bright, and with a kind of fierceness, on old Roger Chillingworth. "Not to thee! But, if it be the soul's disease, then do I commit myself to the one Physician of the soul! He, if it stand with his good pleasure, can cure; or he can kill! . . . But who are thou, that meddlest in this matter?"

Beyond the general tenor of the language, specific phrases from the KJV appear throughout *The Scarlet Letter*: *hold thy peace, stained with sin, yielding up his breath, hearken unto me, fallen into the pit, it came to pass, daily bread, take no thought, stood in the midst.*

But Hawthorne's imagination was so thoroughly influenced by the Bible that the presence of the Bible is felt in the very construction of key episodes in the story. Like Milton, Hawthorne was adept at composing whole scenes on the basis of single Bible verses. The guilt-induced physical decline of Rev. Dimmesdale is an extended narrative example of the truth summarized in Psalm 32:3–4: "When I kept silence, my bones waxed old; through my roaring all the day long. For day and night thy hand was heavy upon me." The final confession scene in which Dimmesdale at last attains forgiveness is an outworking of James 5:16: "Confess your faults one to another, . . . that ye may be healed." Those two verses are the axis between which the whole story moves— unconfessed sin as the problem, confessed sin as the antidote.

The famous scaffold scene in which Dimmesdale confesses his sin is a virtual mosaic of King James echoes. As Dimmesdale invites Hester to join him on the scaffold, he begins his address to her, ". . . in the name of Him, so terrible and so merciful, who gives me grace at this last moment, to do what—for my own heavy sin and miserable agony—I withheld myself from doing seven years ago. . . ." Shortly later Dimmesdale says, "Thanks be to Him who led me hither!" Again, "God is merciful." "May God forgive thee," Dimmesdale says to Chillingworth. And Dimmesdale's dying words are, "Had either of these agonies been wanting, I had been lost for ever! Praised be his name! His will be done! Farewell!"

Herman Melville

When we turn to Hawthorne's contemporary Herman Melville (1819–1891), it is hard to know where to begin. In addition to numerous essays on Melville's use of the Bible, two authors have written entire books on the subject, and both confirm that

Melville's personal Bible was a KJV with heavy annotation by Melville in the margins.[15] One of these scholars shows that the number of KJV references increased steadily during the course of Melville's career.[16] Someone else has written that Melville "knew the Bible well, inheriting from his church-going age an almost unconsciously profound biblical awareness that left Scripture the ground on which his mind invariably walked."[17]

Melville's masterpiece *Moby Dick* illustrates the claim from its opening page. The subject of whaling so captivated Melville that he placed a collection of "extracts" on whaling from famous written sources before chapter 1 even gets under way. The list begins with five verses quoted verbatim from the King James Bible. The story itself begins with one of the most famous opening lines in all of literature: "Call me Ishmael," the narrator confides intimately. At once an Old Testament world is evoked in our imaginations. Other characters with biblical names appear as well—Elijah, Captain Bildad, and (towering above them all) Captain Ahab. Regarding the latter we read, "Ahab of old, thou knowest, was a crowned king!" These characters take on a life of their own, and no close correspondence to their biblical original is worked out, but whenever we read a biblical name in *Moby Dick*, the King James Bible lives on in American literature. I should note in passing that not only does the first sentence of the opening chapter take us to the King James Bible; so does the first sentence of the epilogue: "And I only am escaped alone to tell thee" (Job 1:15–19).

"The Bible has been the greatest single influence on our [American] literature. Our writers, almost without exception, have been steeped in biblical imagery, phrasing, rhythms." —Randall Stewart, *American Literature and Christian Doctrine*

The chapter in *Moby Dick* where the KJV most directly announces its presence is chapter 9, which recounts Father Mapple's sermon on Jonah preached at Whalemen's Chapel, where sailors were accustomed to attending a service before embarking for the high seas. The sermon is a *tour de force* of colloquial preaching, with Father Mapple embellishing and expounding upon the biblical story. Though there are few direct quotations from the book of Jonah, the biblical text continuously surfaces for any reader familiar with the King James Bible, as in the following excerpt:

> The frightened master comes to him, and shrieks in his dead ear, "What meanest thou, O sleeper! Arise!" . . . How furiously they mob him with their questions. "What is thine occupation? Whence comest thou? Thy country? What people?" . . . "I am a Hebrew," he cries—and then—"I fear the Lord the God of Heaven who hath made the sea and the dry land!"

One of the most discussed aspects of *Moby Dick* is the white whale, and a focus of the discussion has been the attempt to identify the likely biblical precedents for Melville's whale. One school of thought links the whale to the Leviathan portrayed by the voice from the whirlwind in the book of Job. The other interpretation believes that Melville's model is the whale of the Old Testament story of Jonah. Probably both biblical texts should be in our awareness as we read, and in both cases the King James Bible weaves its presence throughout Melville's novel.

Sources of a writer's style are difficult to prove, but if a writer's style reminds us of the King James Bible, and if parallels can be demonstrated, it is a fair inference that the KJV has influenced the writer's style. One expert on Melville claims that "his elaborate allusions to the King James Version . . . are accompanied by numerous minute echoes of the particular idioms and textures of this canonical translation."[18] An excerpt from the chapter in *Moby Dick* in which Melville describes the residents of Nantucket illustrates the point:

> The Nantucketer, he alone resides and riots on the sea; he alone, in Bible language, goes down to it in ships; to and fro ploughing

it as his own special plantation. There is his home; there lies his business, which a Noah's flood would not interrupt, though it overwhelmed all the millions in China. He lives on the sea; . . . he hides among the waves, he climbs them. . . .

Alfred, Lord Tennyson

A quick glimpse into the attitude of English Victorian poet Alfred, Lord Tennyson (1809–1892) comes from the *Memoir* that his son Hallam wrote about his father. Hallam claims, "That my father was a student of the Bible, those who have read 'In Memoriam' know. He also eagerly read all notable works within his reach relating to the Bible."[19] Additionally, Hallam tells us that his father thought it valuable to read the Authorized Version "for the sake of the grand English in which it is written."[20] There are more allusions to the Bible in Tennyson's poetry than to any other source.[21]

Tennyson's most famous poem was written late in life after Tennyson had recently recovered from a serious illness. It is entitled "Crossing the Bar" and takes as its subject the contemplation of one's own death and the hope of immortality. Whenever I read the poem, I feel as though I have entered the same world as the King James Bible. The opening verse of the four-stanza lyric is as follows:

> Sunset and evening star,
> And one clear call for me!
> And may there be no moaning of the bar,
> When I put out to sea.

The movement of the lines is exactly like the biblical verse form of parallelism. The first two lines fall into the pattern of synonymous parallelism (the same basic content repeated in different images), while the second pair are an example of synthetic ("growing") parallelism, in which the second line completes the thought of the preceding line. The imagery (sunset, night, star, sea) is also consonant with the King James Bible—at once simple and grand in its archetypes.

The concluding stanza of the poem asserts the spirit that Paul expresses in 2 Timothy 4:6–8, with its phrases "the time of my departure is at hand," having "finished my course," and receiving "a crown of righteousness, which the Lord the righteous judge shall give me at that day."[22] Here is Tennyson's parallel:

> For though from out our bourne [boundary] of Time
> and Place
> The flood may bear me far,
> I hope to see my Pilot face to face
> When I have crossed the bar.

The image of the flood bearing a person away is a commonplace in the Psalms (e.g., 32:6; 69:2; 90:5; 124:4), while the phrase *face to face* quotes one of the most evocative phrases in the whole Bible—"but then face to face" (1 Cor. 13:12).

Most Victorian writers were as indebted to the King James Bible as Tennyson was. Here are specimen quotations:

- "[Charles] Dickens alludes to the [King James] Bible and the Book of Common Prayer more often than to any other texts." —Janet L. Larson, *Dickens and the Broken Scripture*
- "Like Thomas Carlyle and John Ruskin, [novelist George] Eliot absorbed the language of the King James translation so thoroughly as to make it a part of her idiom and manner of thinking." —Charles LaPorte, in *The Blackwell Companion to the Bible in English Literature*
- "Many of [Robert] Browning's poems cannot be thoroughly comprehended without an acquaintance with the Scriptures of the Old and New Testaments . . . and especially with our King James's Version." —Minnie Gresham Machen, *The Bible in Browning*

Tennyson's major work is *In Memoriam*, a collection of 131 lyrics (along with a prologue and epilogue) occasioned by the death of Tennyson's close friend Arthur Henry Hallam. The following critical judgment is exactly right: "*In Memoriam* is infused with biblical language and imagery, so that even when a direct allusion is not apparent Tennyson's words hold religious overtones."[23] The opening stanza of the prologue is a good test case:

> Strong Son of God, immortal Love,
>   Whom we, that have not seen thy face,
>   By faith and faith alone, embrace,
> Believing where we cannot prove.

If we ask what in that stanza reminds us of the English Bible, the answer depends partly on what English Bible we ourselves use. For someone who knows only modern colloquial English Bibles, the stanza evokes much less biblical awareness than it does for someone raised on the KJV or a modern successor like the ESV.

What does Tennyson's opening stanza possess that is reminiscent of the King James Bible? Stateliness and exaltation, first of all. The opening line is formal, consisting of two imposing epithets for God. The syntax, too, is long and flowing, consisting of single invocation to God, and not even self-contained (the sentence is completed in the ensuing stanza). But paradoxically this dignity and exaltation combine with a directness and simplicity that reminds us of the King James Bible.

Additionally, the quoted stanza is a pastiche of famous biblical verses. "Son of God" is a stock epithet for Christ that appears approximately fifty times in the KJV. When Tennyson was asked what he meant by the title "immortal Love," he directed his questioner to 1 John 4:8: "God is love." The statements that we "have not seen thy face" but embrace Christ "by faith" are a reference to Jesus' statement to Thomas that "blessed are they that have not seen, and yet have believed" (John 20:29). And the concluding line of Tennyson's opening stanza—"Believing where we cannot prove"—alludes to Hebrews 11:1: "Now faith is the substance of things hoped for, the evidence of things not seen."

Obviously this density of reference to the KJV does not persist throughout the whole of *In Memoriam*. But as a stylistic influence it is omnipresent, and specific references to the King James Bible are plentiful.

Summary

The authors surveyed in this chapter are representative literary figures from the nineteenth century. The influence of the King James Bible on nineteenth-century English and American literature could as well have been illustrated by Percy Shelley, Lord Byron, Henry David Thoreau, Ralph Waldo Emerson, Charles Dickens, and Robert Browning. In fact, all of these authors have had whole books written on their use of the Bible.[24]

Further Reading

David Lyle Jeffrey, ed., *A Dictionary of Biblical Tradition in English Literature* (1992), 937–60; bibliography of Bible usage, arranged alphabetically by author.

Bruce M. Metzger and M. D. Coogan, eds., *The Oxford Companion to the Bible* (1993), 438–60.

Nancy M. Tischler, *Thematic Guide to Biblical Literature* (2007).

Rebecca Lemon et al., eds., *The Blackwell Companion to the Bible in English Literature* (2009).

15

THE MODERN ERA

In a century [i.e., the twentieth] . . . that has declared itself frequently and vigorously to be secular, . . . the Bible has become . . . a repository of points of reference, of images and allusions, a treasure-house of . . . characters, ideas, narrative modes and patterns into which novelists and poets dip continuously. . . . The Bible remains . . . the most pervasive source-book for twentieth-century authors across many countries.

—DAVID BEVAN, *Literature and the Bible*

IT MIGHT BE EXPECTED that the literary influence of the King James Bible would wane as we move into the modern era, when most English and American authors do not profess the Christian faith. But this is not what we find. Even in the modern era, the Bible is the most referenced book in English and American literature. As I pursue the evidences of this, it is important to restate that I am tracing the history not of Christian belief but of the King James Bible. We also need to be aware that until the mid-twentieth century the KJV was the only widely used Bible among English-speaking authors and readers, and that even after

211

the advent of modern translations, literary authors and scholars have shunned the new translations.

Virginia Woolf and James Joyce

I will begin my survey with two fiction writers who were not professing Christians. Virginia Woolf (1882–1941) was raised in an agnostic home and was ostensibly an atheist. In view of that, her relationship to the Bible is truly surprising. In her *Diary* she makes repeated references to reading the Bible, and additionally she incorporates quotations from the Bible into her diary entries.[1] An example of the latter is her quotation from Psalm 100: "It is He that has made us, not we ourselves. I like that text."[2]

Elsewhere Woolf expresses positive sentiments about the King James Bible. Her highest praise of Thomas Hardy's characters is that "their speech had a Biblical dignity and poetry."[3] The KJV, wrote Woolf, is "a translation of singular beauty," and we cannot deny that its words are "words of the most profound meaning."[4] Again, "the Bible is a work of the greatest interest, much beauty, and deep meaning."[5]

The Bible enters Woolf's fiction at the most general level possible: it supplies a metanarrative or mythological framework for the story line and imaginative world of her stories. While it is hard to prove that this comes directly from the Bible, it is standard procedure for critics to make that assumption.[6] Woolf's 1925 novel *Mrs. Dalloway* provides a good illustration. This is a prevailingly dark story that ends with intimations of renewal in the lives of several characters. The general pattern is a movement from paradisal innocence through fall to redemption through human sacrifice.[7]

"A measure of the literary power of the 'English' Bible in overcoming religious considerations is the complete dominance of the King James Version from its first publication until well into the twentieth century; even James Joyce, who makes copious use of the Bible, prefers the cadences of this English translation to facilitate his inversions." —David Lyle Jeffrey, *The Oxford Companion to the Bible*

James Joyce (1882–1941, identical to the birth and death years of Virginia Woolf) was raised as an Irish Catholic but repudiated that faith as a religion to which he was personally committed. We might think that this eliminates the English Bible as a significant ingredient in his stories, but as with most other major modern English-speaking authors, this presumption turns out to be wrong. A book-length study entitled *Joyce and the Bible* explores echoes and parallels between Joyce's major fiction and the Bible, with the author concluding that for Joyce "the Bible must have been . . . a veritable cornerstone."[8]

Several external considerations immediately confirm the plausibility of what I have said. Joyce's brother claimed that Joyce regarded Dante even more highly than Shakespeare, which is the context within which we can assess the comment that Joyce himself made to his tutor in Italian: "I love Dante almost as much as the Bible."[9] Additionally, anyone who picks up Joyce's mammoth novel *Ulysses* can see at a glance that while Joyce's primary framework comes from Homer's *Odyssey*, once we get beyond the foregrounded Homeric references, we can discern that the Bible is intertwined with those references. The list of biblical names in *Ulysses* runs to nearly six dozen, and the total number of biblical allusions to five hundred.[10]

But of course we need to ask what English translations provided Joyce's biblical knowledge. As a Catholic, Joyce would naturally have absorbed biblical content through both the Catholic liturgy and the Douay Version (supplemented by the Latin Vulgate). But this is not the complete picture. Fifteen of the biblical names in *Ulysses* are specifically from the KJV and three from Douay, with the remaining ones being shared by those two translations.[11] Even more important is the fact that before writing his early autobiographical novel *Stephen Hero*, Joyce copied the entire book of Revelation from the King James Bible into his notebooks.[12] Additionally, the presence of the KJV in English and American literature depends not only on the authors who produced the literature but also on literary critics who oversee the academic study of that literature. When the author of the book on Joyce and the Bible uses the King James Bible throughout her book, the KJV becomes an ingredient in how teachers and students understand Joyce's indebtedness to the Bible.

Joyce's short story "Araby" provides a modest glimpse into how Joyce incorporates the Bible into his fiction. The overall pattern in the story is a fall from innocence, in the sense that a boy's youthful romantic idealism ends in defeat and despair. The second paragraph in the story describes the waste room of the house where the youthful protagonist lives, and also the "wild garden" behind the house. To make sure that we see the link to early Genesis, Joyce includes the detail that there was "a central apple-tree" in the untended back yard.

From the opening we can fast-forward to the story's conclusion. The youthful protagonist arrives at the bazaar where he hopes to buy a love token for his beloved just as it is closing. Within the logic of the story, the bazaar has qualities of a sacred place and is accordingly compared to a church. But this sacred place is desecrated by "two men [who] were counting money," like the moneychangers in the temple (Matt. 21:12–13). More explicitly, as the boy hero of the story stands paralyzed while looking at the vases in a stall, we read that "the great jars . . . stood like eastern guards at either side of the dark entrance to the stall." The story of the fall enters our awareness, in particular Genesis 3:24: "So he drove out the man: and he placed at the East of the Garden of Eden, Cherubims, and a flaming sword, which turned every way, to keep the way of the tree of life."

Ernest Hemingway and John Steinbeck

Ernest Hemingway (1889–1961) had a Protestant upbringing with ample exposure to the Bible. Hemingway's literary friend John Dos Passos claimed that "Ernest and I used to read the Bible to each other," adding that Hemingway "began it."[13] Although no book-length study of Hemingway and the Bible exists, the writer of an essay offers the opinion that "it is clearly the subject for a book."[14]

A good starting point is the novel for which Hemingway took the title straight from the Bible—*The Sun Also Rises*. An author who pins a Bible verse on the title page of a novel in that very act decisively plants an interpretive flag on the territory represented by the ensuing novel. *The Sun Also Rises* is the title that a publisher encouraged Hemingway to adopt for his 1926 novel. But the tie between the novel and the Old Testament book of Ecclesiastes goes deeper than the title. Hemingway placed two epigraphs before the title page. One is a statement that novelist Gertrude Stein had expressed in a conversation with Hemingway: "You are all a lost generation." Immediately following, Hemingway printed the following from Ecclesiastes 1:4–7:

> One generation passeth away, and another generation cometh; but the earth abideth forever. The sun also ariseth, and the sun goeth down, and hasteth to the place where he arose. The wind goeth toward the south, and turneth about unto the north; it whirleth about continually, and the wind returneth again according to his circuits. All the rivers run into the sea; yet the sea is not full; unto the place from whence the rivers come, thither they return again.

It is obvious at once that this passage is coming straight from the King James Bible (although Hemingway changed the archaic *riseth* to *rises* for the title). Later in life Hemingway claimed that the passage from Ecclesiastes was intended to soften and balance the statement by Gertrude Stein. The quoted passage from Ecclesiastes does not yield quite that simple a view, but that need not concern us here. What matters is that we enter Hemingway's novel through the portal of a passage from the KJV, and further that every time we turn a page of the novel, the running head at the top of the page flashes the King James Bible onto our awareness as a presiding presence in the novel.

A biblical title and epigraph represent a localized instance of the Bible's influence on Hemingway. If we move to the global level, we enter the sphere of deep-structure narrative patterns and symbolism. The Hemingway story with which critics have seen the most biblical influence is his novelette *The Old Man and the Sea.*[15] Here we find such biblical elements as a biblical name (Santiago, Spanish for Saint James), references to events in the Gospels (such as an echoing of the time when Jesus told his disciples to "launch out into the deep" in order to catch fish), playing with the words *faith* and *hope* in such a way as to evoke biblical echoes, images that gesture toward the crucifixion and resurrection stories in the Gospels, and an underlying archetypal pattern of death and rebirth (or the Christian paradox of gaining by losing). Analysis of *For Whom the Bell Tolls* has yielded similar results.[16]

We can also see a biblical influence on Hemingway's prose style. Hemingway is famous for his crisp, relatively simple prose style, offset with occasional flourishes and rhetorical patterns. John Dos Passos claimed that Hemingway's preference for short sentences was based on the King James Bible.[17] A literary critic claims that in Hemingway "a purely colloquial modern English and an English which belongs in its essence to the King James version of the Bible are brought together to mutual advantage."[18]

"That Hemingway was influenced by the Bible in matters of craft is clear from his use of simple narrative, repetition and poetry. . . . [In] its appropriation of images directly or indirectly related to both the Testaments, and its frequent adoptions of the rhythms of the King James Bible, the Hemingway short story demonstrates a closeness with the Authorized Version." —Ajanta Paul, "Biblical Resonances in Hemingway's Short Fiction"

In *The Grapes of Wrath*, "Steinbeck quotes Biblical texts, subtly or significantly changes phrases, employs direct or inverted images, and consciously or unconsciously narrates a parallel story [to the Old Testament Exodus]. So fundamental and so extensive is the Biblical imagery that it cannot be regarded as either accidental or incidental." —J. R. C. Perkin, "Exodus Imagery in *The Grapes of Wrath*"

Whereas the biblical element in Hemingway is subtle and subsurface, in John Steinbeck (1902–1968) the biblical presence is overt. A clue to this comes from a document late in Steinbeck's literary career—his Nobel Prize acceptance speech (1962). A leading theme in the speech is the indictment that modern humanity has "usurped many of the powers we once ascribed to God." To clinch the point, Steinbeck parodied the Christ hymn that stands at the beginning of the Gospel of John: "So that today, St. John the apostle may well be paraphrased: In the end is the Word, and the Word is Man—and the Word is with Men." This readiness to refer to the King James Bible is a vintage Steinbeck trait.

The degree to which Steinbeck wished his ties to the Bible to be apparent is suggested most overtly by the fact that he took four titles from the Bible. The most direct is the novelette entitled *The Pearl*, which references Jesus' parable of the pearl of great price (Matt. 13:45–46). Nearly as direct is the title of Steinbeck's 1932 novel *To a God Unknown*, which references the Athenian inscription that Paul noted in his speech to the Areopagus (Acts 17:23). The third biblical title is *The Grapes of Wrath*, which alludes to two biblical passages—Isaiah 63:3 and Revelation 14:19–20. Both passages highlight the image of God's treading a winepress of wrath. Finally, *East of Eden* is a verbatim quotation of the last phrase of the story of Cain and Abel: "And Cain went out from the presence of the LORD, and dwelt in the land of Nod, on the East of Eden" (Gen. 4:16).

But the titles are only the beginning of the indebtedness of these stories to the Bible. The biblical allusions and echoes in *The Grapes of Wrath* have been explored in dozens of critical essays. We can start with names: Noah Joad, Jim Casy (with many parallels to Jesus Christ), Rosasharn ("Rose of Sharon"). The journey of the Joad family from Oklahoma to California is managed by Steinbeck in such a way as to suggest the Exodus of the Israelites to a Promised Land. Twelve family members undertake the journey from a land of oppression, corresponding to the number of tribes that left Egypt. Tom Joad emerges as a Moses-type leader of the traveling clan. Literary critics have uncovered so many parallels that *The Grapes of Wrath* takes shape as a vast network (almost a crossword puzzle) of biblical references.[19]

East of Eden is even more directly linked with the Bible. In this novel Steinbeck retells the story of Cain and Abel in a modern setting. The main motif carried over from Genesis is sibling rivalry between two brothers whose father is Adam Trask. More specific parallels leap out, such as Charles Trask's scar, of which he says, "It just seems like I was marked," or the sneer of the elder brother Cal, "Am I supposed to look out for him?" when Adam asks were his younger brother has gone. But the most significant biblical element in *East of Eden* is the discussion of the biblical story of Cain and Abel that occurs among characters in the novel. In effect, Steinbeck the novelist becomes Steinbeck the biblical interpreter.

The dialogue occurs in chapter 22 and begins with one of the characters reading snatches of Genesis 4 straight from the KJV: "Adam knew Eve his wife; and she conceived, and bare Cain" (v. 4). The entire biblical text is then read in its King James form. A section of dialogue ensues in which various characters comment on the story of Cain and Abel as told in the Bible. Eventually the character named Lee becomes really cogent on the story of Cain and Abel, calling it "the best-known story in the world because it is everybody's story"—in fact "the symbol story of the human soul." This story of rejection, says Lee, is "a chart of the soul—the secret, rejected, guilty soul." The discussion began when someone arrived to help name newborn twin boys, and after the discussion a series of biblical names is suggested from the story of Exodus—Caleb, Joshua, Aaron.

T. S. Eliot

Whereas the biblical element in the four authors discussed above is implicit and latent, T. S. Eliot (1888–1965) is in the lineage of writers like Herbert, Milton, and Bunyan—authors whose work is permeated by the Bible. T. S. Eliot was such a vigorous defender of the Authorized Version against contemporary translations that we can guess a priori what English Bible he used, but we can get a quick glimpse into Eliot the Bible reader from the epigraph that stands at the head of his poem "The Hippopotamus": "And when this epistle is read among you, cause that it be read also in the church of the Laodiceans" (Col. 4:16).

Eliot's Christmas poem *Journey of the Magi* illustrates pretty much the full range of options laid out in chapter 12 (above). The story of the journey of wise men or magi to pay homage to the Christ child in Bethlehem (Matt. 2:1–12) is the source of Eliot's poem. Eliot makes the story come alive in full vividness, naturally going beyond the few details of the biblical text but nonetheless building upon it as his foundation. In the opening stanza Eliot uses a matter-of-fact enumeration of realistic details in the style of biblical narrative. Additionally, the syntax is kept fluid with the conjunction *and*, which is a hallmark of the Bible in its original and in the KJV tradition of translation:

> And the night-fires going out, and the lack of shelters,
> And the cities hostile and the towns unfriendly
> And the villages dirty and charging high prices.

As we read the stanza, we are moving in the world of the Gospels.

With the second stanza the mode shifts entirely, from realism to conventional Christian and biblical allusions and symbols. The main drift of Eliot's poem is to delineate the sacrificial dimension of Christ's nativity, and the symbols of stanza 2 embody that interpretation. Here are just three lines for purposes of illustration:

> And three trees on the low sky,
> And an old white horse galloped away in the meadow.
> Then we came to a tavern with vine-leaves over the
> lintel.

The three trees silhouetted against the sky transport us in imagination to the scene of the crucifixion. The white horse suggests the picture of Christ as conquering hero on a white horse—battle motif—in Revelation 19:11–14. The vine leaves hint at the wine of communion (Christ's sacrifice), and the phrase *over the lintel* recalls the blood smeared on the door frames of the Israelites on the night of the Passover.

The third and concluding stanza of Eliot's poem leaves the actual journey behind and takes us inside the mind of the narrator as he recalls the journey in his old age. Here the poem becomes a conversion story, as the wise man interprets the revolution that the visit to the Christ child initiated in his life. The language continues to be biblical. The Birth (capitalized by Eliot) was the wise man's Death (also capitalized), evoking the biblical imagery of death to self and sin. The result of this conversion was this:

> We returned to our places, these Kingdoms,
> But no longer at ease here, in the old dispensation,
> With an alien people clutching their gods.

The narrator is the archetypal alien of the New Testament Epistles, looking to a spiritual city whose maker and builder is God. And the picture that he paints of the homeland to which he returned at the end of his journey is the biblical archetype of pagans worshiping false gods.

> "The age covered by the reigns of Elizabeth I and James I was richer in writers of genius than is our own, and we should not expect a translation made in our time to be a masterpiece of our literature or, as was the Authorized Version of 1611, an exemplar of English prose for successive generations of writers. . . . Nothing will be gained [by the introduction of the New English Bible], for the new version will be just as hard to grasp, when read in church, as the Authorized Version, and it will lack the verbal beauty of the Authorized Version." —T. S. Eliot, review of New English Bible

Eliot's play *Murder in the Cathedral* exhibits all of these biblical traits on a grand scale. This play was commissioned by the Friends of Canterbury Cathedral and first performed on the cathedral grounds in 1935, which perhaps explains why Eliot chose the martyrdom of Thomas á Becket as his story material. The execution is thoroughly biblical in flavor, and the presence of the King James Bible, specifically, throughout the play is partly explained by a conclusion that was reached at a weekend conference attended by organizers of the annual drama festival in Canterbury. It was agreed by the planners "that the Authorized Version of the Bible was especially suitable for text as well as subject of religious plays."[20]

Murder in the Cathedral fits this paradigm. The organizing format comes from the New Testament Gospels. At the center of the action is a Christian martyr who dies an atoning death—not atoning as Christ's atonement was, but in the sense that Becket's death is the means by which the chorus (the poor women of Canterbury) come to saving faith. Around this central figure are a group of priests, who interact with Thomas as the disciples did with Jesus. Beyond this inner circle is a band of murderous conspirators and a group of onlookers who must interact with the scenes of conflict between the protagonist and his oppressors. The martyr undergoes a series of temptations that parallel Christ's temptations.

This central action based on the Bible is accompanied by a poetic texture that regularly advertises its biblical origin. For example, the third priest offers the sentiment that the wheel of fortune should be allowed to turn

> Until the grinders cease
> And the door shall be shut in the street,
> And all the daughters of music shall be brought low.

The images and phrases are coming from the KJV rendition of the portrait of an aging person near the end of the book of Ecclesiastes (12:3–4): "the grinders cease, because they are few"; "the doors shall be shut in the streets"; "all the daughters of music shall be brought low."

Again, the fourth tempter, in tempting Thomas to do the right thing (accept martyrdom) for the wrong reason, says to Thomas, "And see far off below you, where the gulf is fixed, your persecutors, in timeless torment." This has been imported from Jesus' parable of the rich man and Lazarus (Luke 16:19–31): "And in hell [the rich man] lift up his eyes being in torments, and seeth Abraham afar off, and Lazarus in his bosom. . . . And besides all this, between us and you there is a great gulf fixed." Some of the biblical references are more latent than this. The play ends with a choral speech that follows the format of the Old Testament psalms of praise. The controlling motif is stated at the outset, and it has the "feel" of a biblical psalm of praise: "We praise Thee, O God, for Thy glory displayed in all the creatures of the earth."

Modern Poetry

To fill out the picture of the literary influence of the King James Bible in modern literature, I will balance the foregoing portraits of five major authors with a wide-angle view of poetry and then of the novel. A good starting point for modern poetry is an anthology entitled *The Gospels in Our Image: An Anthology of Twentieth-Century Poetry Based on Biblical Texts.*[21] The anthology runs to 250 pages of Gospel passages and modern poems based on them. Although the editor chose the RSV rather than the KJV for the passages from the Gospels, he made that choice because the RSV "is written in a contemporary style that still preserves almost all the phrases and cadences of the King James Version that have entered the English literary tradition and are often quoted or alluded to in the poems." Many of the poems in the anthology come from the "heavyweights" of modern poetry—William Butler Yeats, D. H. Lawrence, Philip Larkin, W. H. Auden, Dylan Thomas.

American poet Edwin Arlington Robinson (1869–1935), hailed at the time of his death as America's preeminent poet, was primarily a poet of despair. We might therefore predict that the Bible would be absent from his poetry, but the persistence of the Bible even in such rocky soil proves the point of this chapter. Biographer Scott Donaldson claims that "the Bible . . . was his greatest source."[22] Donaldson also writes that "three books . . . always lay on his work table: the Bible, a collected Shakespeare, and the dictionary. The Bible provided him with much of the material he fashioned into poems."[23]

The result is that a dozen titles in Robinson's *Collected Poems* are taken from the Bible, including "Many Are Called," "The Valley of the Shadow," "Peace on Earth," "Sisera," "Young Gideon," and "The Prodigal Son." The poem entitled "The Three Taverns" (which Robinson also made the title of one of his books of poems) is preceded by an epigraph consisting of a verbatim quotation of Acts 18:15 from the King James Bible.

Robert Frost (1874–1963) presents a similar picture— someone whose indebtedness to the Bible is literary rather than religious. Frost was capable of using the Bible as a source for the content of a work: his drama *Masque of Reason* takes its story line from the book of Job, and his companion piece *Masque of Mercy* takes its central situation from the book of Jonah. Frost's most famous poems employ a simple and somewhat archaic diction, combined with solemnity of tone, that one critic calls "the tradition of simple elevation," of which the "arch-exemplar is the Authorized Version of the Bible."[24] Someone else claims that "Frost loved the Scriptures and . . . was soaked in the King James version."[25]

> "The imaginations of many of the major 20th century writers have been gripped by the power of these great biblical patterns. . . . Modern authors use the 'living structures' of the Bible as 'outlines,' as conceptualized patterns for their human concerns in their art." —Marion Fairman, *Biblical Patterns in Modern Literature*

The King James Bible has been the preferred English Bible of the African-American community, and James Weldon Johnson (1871–1938) can be taken as representative. Johnson was an extraordinarily versatile person for whom writing was an avocation, and even within the literary sphere, he wrote in multiple genres. Still, Johnson's "signature work" is surely his volume of poems entitled *God's Trombones* and subtitled *Seven Negro Sermons in Verse*. These poems capture the vocabulary and cadence of black preaching in America. Johnson himself tells us how the King James Bible fits into the picture in his preface to the volume: when the "old-time Negro preachers" preached, they "stepped out" from the "narrow confines" of their everyday dialect. In their preaching style, they were all "steeped in the idioms of King James English, so when they preached and warmed to their work they spoke another language." The result is "a fusion of Negro idioms with Bible English."[26]

This is exactly what we find in the seven "sermons" that make up *God's Trombones*. The following specimen from "Noah Built the Ark" captures the flavor of the whole:

> But Noah was a just and righteous man.
> Noah walked and talked with God.
> And, one day, God said to Noah,
> He said: Noah, build thee an ark.
> Build it out of gopher wood.
> Build it good and strong.
> Pitch it within and pitch it without.

We should note finally that the King James Bible can suddenly pop up in the poetry of writers whom we would not consider rooted in the Bible. "I will arise and go," we read in the opening line of William Butler Yeats's poem "The Lake Isle of Innisfree," and we immediately recognize the quotation from the parable of the prodigal son (Luke 15:18), as well as God's command to Jonah (1:2). "And Death Shall Have No Dominion," Dylan Thomas entitled a poem, a quotation from Romans 6:9. "The race is not to the swift," reads the first line of D. H. Lawrence's poem "Race and Battle," in direct quotation of Ecclesiastes 9:11. The speaker in Thomas Hardy's poem "The Darkling Thrush" theorizes that the singing thrush must know "Some blessed Hope," in echo of "that blessed hope" of Titus 2:13.

The Modern Novel

A random survey of novelists akin to the survey of poets will complete this excursion into the continuing influence of the King James Bible on modern literature. American novelist William Faulkner (1897–1962) is a good place to begin. Faulkner signaled his link to the Bible by pinning a biblical name on two of his novels—*Absalom, Absalom!* based on King David's lament for his dead son, and *Go Down, Moses*, based on God's call of Moses in the Old Testament epic of the exodus. But these are only like a billboard on the highway. The more subtle presence of the Bible in Faulkner's fiction has been traced in dozens of essays and book chapters. The author of a book on Faulkner and the Bible identifies "approximately 379 verses or combinations identifiable in Faulkner's nineteen novels as being taken from the King James version of the Bible."[27]

The rootedness of Polish-born British novelist Joseph Conrad (1857–1924) in the Bible has produced a book-length study.[28] This book shows that the biblical presence in Conrad's fiction consists primarily of direct quotations from the Bible and allusions to it. In the conclusion to the book, the author demonstrates that "the King James version . . . is incontestably the source" of Conrad's biblical references, and then he offers this final statement: "In the English Bible Conrad found a way to enter the traditions of English literature. . . . Without the English Bible, Conrad could not have been the writer we know."[29]

William Golding (1911–1993) wrote a novel that has been a classic for generations of students enrolled in high school English classes. It is entitled *Lord of the Flies*, and tracing the biblical allusions and symbols in it is so customary in school courses that it is a virtual rite of passage. The title itself comes straight from the Bible, being a translation of the name Beelzebub—in the Old Testament a Philistine god and in the New Testament Satan, or "the prince of demons." When we turn from the title of the novel to the chapter titles, we find more biblical borrowings: "Fire on the Mountain" (multiple biblical passages) and "Beast from Water" (Rev. 13:1). The story line of a fall from innocence in a paradisal setting comes from Genesis 3. Beyond these broad outlines, critics have found an ever-expanding network of biblical echoes and symbols.

Like many twentieth-century authors, Toni Morrison (1931–) has been the subject of an entire book on the use of the Bible in her novels.[30] And like other major novelists, Morrison has taken some of her novel titles from the Bible (*Song of Solomon* and *Paradise*). Fictional characters sometimes bear biblical names—Magdalene, Ruth, Pilate, and Hagar in *Song of Solomon*, for example. Mainly, though, Morrison evokes the Bible not to signal her compliance with its belief system but rather to create what literary critics call an intertext in which the important meaning resides in the interplay between the preexisting text—the Bible—and the new work of fiction.

Of course we need to ascertain what English Bible fuels all these submerged biblical elements. The epigraph that stands at the very head of Morrison's novel *Beloved* tells us what we need to know: "I will call them my people, which were not my people; and her beloved, which was not beloved" (Rom. 9:25, KJV). When an interviewer said to Morrison, "When I began *Song of Solomon* I thought, the King James Bible is the spine of this style," Morrison implicitly accepted the assessment by replying, "The Bible wasn't part of my reading, it was part of my life."[31]

As a postscript, I will note that even in really contemporary novels, when we might expect an author's allegiance to have gravitated from the KJV to a more recent translation, the King James Bible is still the most frequently used English Bible. By the time we reach page 37 of Marilynne Robinson's *Gilead* (2004), we read, "The full soul loatheth an honeycomb; but to the hungry soul every bitter thing is sweet" (Prov. 27:7).[32] Near the end of the novel we read, "The Lord make His face to shine upon thee and be gracious unto thee: The Lord lift up His countenance upon thee, and give thee peace" (Num. 6:25–26). Similarly in Barbara Kingsolver's *The Poisonwood Bible* (1998) each of the seven "books" into which the novel is divided is preceded by a title page that bears an epigraph taken straight from the KJV, such as this one: "And ye shall make no league with the inhabitants of this land; ye shall throw down their altars" (Judg. 2:2).

Summary

The authors surveyed in this chapter are representative figures. An alternate set of major authors would have yielded the same picture of the continuing influence of the King James Bible on English and American literature. Even though the Bible no longer elicits the religious belief of most authors, the King James Bible has remained a pervasive literary presence.

Further Reading

Roland Bartel, ed., *Biblical Images in Literature* (1975).

David Lyle Jeffrey, ed., *A Dictionary of Biblical Tradition in English Literature* (1992), 937–60; bibliography of Bible usage, arranged alphabetically by author.

David Curzon, ed., *The Gospels in Our Image: An Anthology of Twentieth-Century Poetry Based on Biblical Texts* (1995).

Rebecca Lemon et al., eds., *The Blackwell Companion to the Bible in English Literature* (2009).

Robert Alter, *Pen of Iron: American Prose and the King James Bible* (2010).

AFTERWORD

I HAVE TOLD THE STORY OF THE KING JAMES BIBLE from its origin to the present day. It is natural to ask how we should regard the KJV today, and what future remains for the esteemed King James tradition. I propose that we should celebrate a victory, lament a loss, and resolve to hold on to what is excellent.

Celebrating a Victory

In the preceding chapters I have told the story of the triumph of the King James Bible. The major landmarks in that story include the literary excellence of the KJV itself, its relatively quick acceptance as the best English translation of the Bible, its predominant use by English-speaking Christians for over three centuries, and its status as virtually the sole biblical influence on British and American culture even to the present day. This should be a cause for gratitude and celebration, regardless of one's preferred English Bible translation at the present moment.

Lamenting a Loss

What has been lost with the diminished presence of the King James Bible in English-speaking Christendom? At least four things.

First, we have lost a common English Bible in both the church and culture at large. It is an incalculable loss. On numerous fronts, life was greatly simplified when virtually everyone agreed on what was meant by "the Bible." Conversely, many things became problematical when that agreement ceased, and some things were permanently lost (see below).

Second, the authority of the Bible went into eclipse when we lost a common Bible. Probably this was inevitable, but we do not need to explore the logic of that line of thought here. It is a fact that the English Bible is no longer accepted as an authoritative book in the public spheres that I have explored in this book—religion, education, law, politics, and the arts. Even when modern literary authors refer to the Bible, they usually do so in a manner that challenges the intended meanings of the biblical authors.

Third, biblical illiteracy has accompanied the decline of the King James Bible. This is widely acknowledged. When a colleague in my own department learned that I was writing a book on the King James Bible and its legacy, she volunteered the observation that after the King James Bible gave way to a proliferation of modern translations, even Christian students became inept at seeing biblical references in literature. Recently the media were abuzz with a volley shot by Andrew Motion, Poet Laureate of England, about contemporary students' inability to detect biblical allusions in literature courses. Motion said in a BBC interview that today's students know so little of the Bible that when he recently taught Milton's *Paradise Lost*, "It was very difficult even to get beyond go in talking about it."[1]

Claims by modern translators and Bible scholars that the Christian public is fortunate to have been delivered from the archaisms and occasional inaccuracies of the KJV turn out to be hollow. If Bible knowledge in our day has declined across the board, where is the alleged gain from modern translations? The very proliferation of translations has discouraged the Christian public from seeking to know what the Bible actually says. The ideal, of course, would have been for a single successor to the KJV to be its replacement, but it did not happen.

The sentiment is widely held that because today we find the King James Bible archaic and difficult, it must have been equally archaic and difficult for readers in previous eras. It is a great fallacy. Readers of the KJV through the centuries did not struggle with its language, just as modern readers who never relinquished the KJV manage just fine with it. Are we better off today without the KJV than Christendom was for three centuries with it? No: those eras had many advantages over us. Although we cannot turn back the clock, we should lament what has been lost, not claim an illusory superiority.

What has been lost? A common English Bible, a nearly universal reverence for the Bible as an authoritative book, and biblical literacy. Finally, we have lost the affective and literary power of the King James Bible—not in an absolute sense, inasmuch as the RSV, NKJV, and ESV do a wonderful job of approximating the qualities of the KJV in updated English vocabulary. But approximation is not duplication. Of course dynamic equivalent and colloquial translations do not come close to the King James standard, and modern readers of those translations have no reason to gloat; they have exchanged a birthright of excellence for something manifestly inferior.

Holding On to What Is Excellent

What does the King James Bible of 1611 offer to us as we look to the future? For those who honor the King James Bible, the legacy is a living one, in at least four ways.

First, we need to avoid losing sight of an obvious fact: if we consult the figures of Bible sales today, the KJV appears as either the second or third on the list. The publishers of most modern translations would love to be in the position of the KJV. Furthermore, a survey of Internet sites quickly reveals a far-flung subculture of churches, schools, and individuals whose loyalty to the KJV remains unabated. For thousands and probably millions of Bible readers, the King James Version has not suffered an eclipse.

Second, as I showed in chapter 5, the King James Bible endures in modern Bible translations that accept the principles and practices of the King James translators. Except for printing biblical poetry as though it were prose, the KJV is based on the right principles. Again, therefore, we can see that (to adapt a quip by Mark Twain when his death was erroneously reported in a newspaper), rumors of the demise of the KJV have been greatly exaggerated. Next to reading the King James Bible itself, the highest honor conferred on the KJV today is the translations that perpetuate its theory and practice of translation.

Third, now that we know who among literary authors, musical composers, and visual artists used the KJV as their English Bible, we should use the KJV when we interact with their works. There is no excuse for perpetuating the naïve practice of speaking of "the Bible" in connection with the work of these artists, and then quoting from whatever translation we ourselves use. The scholarly enterprise deserves more precision than this.

Finally, even if we use a modern translation *most* of the time, there are good reasons to read the King James Bible *some* of the time. Its qualities are unique. C. S. Lewis claimed that one of the characteristics of a "classic" is that no substitute can take the place of the original. Even the archaic language of the KJV can serve good purposes and need not be regarded only as a difficulty to be tolerated in order to appropriate the advantages of the King James Bible. The archaic language of the King James Bible (a) allows us to exercise continuity with a past that we should treasure and (b) alerts us to the ancientness and "otherness" of the original biblical text.

We should not relegate the King James Bible to the status of a relic in the museum of the past. There are multiple ways in which it can continue to be a living presence in our lives. We can read it. We can choose as our primary English Bible a translation that perpetuates the translation philosophy and style of the KJV. We can use the King James Version when we discuss writers, composers, and artists whose work is rooted in the KJV. The choice is ours. The King James Bible is still sold and available nearly everywhere.

NOTES

Chapter 1: In the Beginning

1. F. F. Bruce, *History of the Bible in English* (New York: Oxford University Press, 1978), 20.

2. John Purvey, Prologue to the Wycliffe Bible, chapter 15 (accessed online at http://www.bible-researcher.com/wyclif2.html).

3. Ibid.

4. Alec Gilmore, *A Dictionary of the English Bible and Its Origins* (Sheffield: Sheffield Academic, 2000), 186.

5. Brian Moynahan, *God's Bestseller: William Tyndale, Thomas More, and the Writing of the English Bible* (New York: St. Martin's, 2002), 106.

6. David Daniell, *The Bible in English: Its History and Influence* (New Haven: Yale University Press, 2003), 158.

Chapter 2: From Tyndale to the King James Bible

1. Henry W. Hamilton-Hoare, *Evolution of the English Bible* (London: John Murray, 1902), 137; Benson Bobrick, *Wide as the Waters: The Story of the English Bible and the Revolution It Inspired* (New York: Penguin, 2001), 96.

2. Bobrick, *Wide as the Waters*, 146.

3. J. Isaacs, "The Sixteenth-Century Versions," in *The Bible in Its Ancient and English Versions*, ed. H. Wheeler Robinson (1940; repr., Westport, CT: Greenwood, 1970), 172.

4. Donald Brake, *A Visual History of the English Bible* (Grand Rapids: Baker, 2008), 127.

5. Ibid., 137.

6. Charles C. Butterworth, *The Literary Lineage of the King James Bible, 1340–1611* (Philadelphia: University of Pennsylvania Press, 1941), 163.

Chapter 3: The Making of the King James Bible

1. Excellent recent books on the making of the King James Bible include the following: Alister McGrath, *In the Beginning: The Story of the King James Bible and How It Changed a Nation, a Language, and a Culture* (New York: Anchor, 2001); Benson Bobrick, *Wide as the Waters: The Story of the English Bible and the Revolution It Inspired* (New York: Penguin, 2001); David Daniell, *The Bible in English: Its History and Influence* (New Haven: Yale University Press, 2003); Adam Nicolson, *God's Secretaries: The Making of the King James Bible* (New York: HarperCollins, 2003). In this chapter, all of my information has come from these books unless otherwise noted.

2. James Baikie, *The English Bible and Its Story* (Philadelphia: J. B. Lippincott, 1959), 258.

3. Ibid., 262.

4. Daniell, *The Bible in English*, 432.

5. Bobrick, *Wide as the Waters*, 218.

6. Ibid., 217.

7. Eugene Peterson, *Eat This Book: A Conversation in the Art of Spiritual Reading* (Grand Rapids: Eerdmans, 2006), 162.

8. Gustavus S. Paine, *The Men Behind the King James Version* (1959; repr., Grand Rapids: Baker, 1977), 41, 167–68.

9. In addition to Bobrick, Nicolson, and Paine, already cited: Olga S. Opfell, *The King James Bible Translators* (Jefferson, NC: McFarland, 1982).

10. Bobrick, *Wide as the Waters*, 217.

11. The chronology of the translation process can be gleaned from sources such as the following: Baikie, *The English Bible and Its Story*, 271; Herbert Gordon May, *Our English Bible in the Making* (Philadelphia: Westminster, 1952), 52; Donald Brake, *A Visual History of the English Bible* (Grand Rapids: Baker, 2008), 191.

12. I have taken the information that I present in this paragraph from Geddes MacGregor, *The Bible in the Making* (Philadelphia: J. B. Lippincott, 1959), 163.

13. Ibid., 181.

14. The figures about numbers of editions in this paragraph come from ibid., 187.

15. McGrath, *In the Beginning*, 284.

16. Data in this paragraph comes from Daniell, *The Bible in English*, 487–88.

17. Ibid., 581. As Daniell traces the unfolding history of the Bible in America, he notes the "unassailable" position of the KJV (632).

18. Ibid., 622.

Chapter 4: The King James Bible of 1611

1. Adam Nicolson, *God's Secretaries: The Making of the King James Bible* (New York: HarperCollins, 2003), 223.

2. Benson Bobrick, *Wide as the Waters: The Story of the English Bible and the Revolution It Inspired* (New York: Penguin, 2001), 239–40, 158.

3. Craig R. Thompson, *The Bible in English, 1525–1611* (Ithaca, NY: Cornell University Press, 1958), 27.

4. Samuel McComb, *The Making of the English Bible* (New York: Moffat, Yard, 1909), 94, 97.

5. M. Ellsworth Olsen, *The Prose of Our King James Version: Its Origin and Course of Development* (Washington, DC: Review and Herald, 1947), 86.

6. Charles C. Butterworth, *The Literary Lineage of the King James Bible, 1340–1611* (Philadelphia: University of Pennsylvania Press, 1941), 242.

7. Edgar J. Goodspeed, *The Making of the English New Testament* (Chicago: University of Chicago Press, 1925), 50.

8. Alister McGrath, *In the Beginning: The Story of the King James Bible and How It Changed a Nation, a Language, and a Culture* (New York: Anchor, 2001), 250.

9. Ibid., 252.

10. Donald Brake, *A Visual History of the English Bible* (Grand Rapids: Baker, 2008), 204.

11. Cleland Boyd McAfee, *The Greatest English Classic* (New York: Harper and Brothers, 1912), 72.

12. As McGrath, *In the Beginning*, 242, correctly notes, "It must be made clear immediately that this does not call into question the general reliability of the King James Bible. The issue concerns minor textual variations. Not a single teaching of the Christian faith is affected by these variations."

13. Albert S. Cook, "The 'Authorized Version' and Its Influence," in *The Cambridge History of English Literature*, 15 vols. (Cambridge: Cambridge University Press, 1933), 4:52.

14. Thomas Babington Macaulay, *The Miscellaneous Writings of Lord Macaulay* (London: Longmans Green, 1868), 118.

15. Nicolson, *God's Secretaries*, 224.

16. Geddes MacGregor, *The Bible in the Making* (Philadelphia: J. B. Lippincott, 1959), 192.

17. McGrath, *In the Beginning*, 300.

18. David Daniell, *The Bible in English: Its History and Influence* (New Haven: Yale University Press, 2003), 427.

19. J. Isaacs, "The Sixteenth-Century Versions," in *The Bible in Its Ancient and English Versions*, ed. H. Wheeler Robinson (1940; repr., Westport, CT: Greenwood, 1970), 204–5.

Chapter 5: The Influence of the King James Bible on the History of Bible Translation

1. Calvin Linton, "The Importance of Literary Style," in *The Making of the NIV*, ed. Kenneth L. Barker (Grand Rapids: Baker, 1991), 26.

2. Eugene Peterson, *Eat This Book: A Conversation in the Art of Spiritual Reading* (Grand Rapids: Eerdmans, 2006), 161.

3. William A. Irwin, "Method and Procedure in the Revision," in Luther A. Weigle et al., *An Introduction to the Revised Standard Version of the Old Testament* (New York: Nelson, 1952), 13–14.

4. Leland Ryken, *The Word of God in English: Criteria for Excellence in Bible Translation* (Wheaton: Crossway, 2002); Ryken, *Understanding English Bible Translation: The Case for an Essentially Literal Approach* (Wheaton: Crossway, 2009).

Chapter 6: The Influence of the King James Bible on Language, Education, and Religion

1. Clifford Geertz, "Ritual and Social Change: A Javanese Example," *American Anthropologist* 59 (1957): 33.

2. All quotations in this paragraph can be found somewhere in Lindbeck's wonderful essay "The Church's Mission to a Postmodern Culture," in *Postmodern Theology: Christian Faith in a Pluralist World*, ed. Frederic B. Burnham (New York: Harper and Row, 1989), 36–55.

3. Alister McGrath, *In the Beginning: The Story of the King James Bible and How It Changed a Nation, a Language, and a Culture* (New York: Anchor, 2001), 153, 259. McGrath also agrees with the majority opinion that "the King James Bible was published within a window of opportunity, which allowed it to exercise a substantial and decisive influence over the shaping of the English language" (258).

4. David Crystal, interview on the King James Bible (accessed online from the Web site Icons of England).

5. William Rosenau, *Hebraisms in the Authorized Version of the Bible* (Baltimore: Friedenwald, 1903), 164.

6. *Bartlett's Bible Quotations* (New York: Little, Brown, 2005).

7. David Daniell, *The Bible in English: Its History and Influence* (New Haven: Yale University Press, 2003), 621–23.

8. McGrath, *In the Beginning*, 290.

9. Benson Bobrick, *Wide as the Waters: The Story of the English Bible and the Revolution It Inspired* (New York: Penguin, 2001), 12.

10. Ype Schaaf, *On Their Way Rejoicing: The History and Role of the Bible in Africa* (Carlisle, UK: Paternoster, 1994), 172.

11. R. S. Sugirtharajah, *The Bible and Empire: Postcolonial Explorations* (Cambridge: Cambridge University Press, 2005), 227; and Sugirtharajah, *The Bible and the Third World: Precolonial, Colonial and Postcolonial Encounters* (Cambridge: Cambridge University Press, 2001), 87, 50.

12. All data in this paragraph is from Marie Friesema, e-mail to the author, May 28, 2009.

13. Vijai John, e-mails to author, May 18 and June 11, 2009.

14. Sam Hsu, e-mail to author, May 26, 2009.

15. Johann Buis, e-mail to author, May 6, 2009.

16. Chinua Achebe, *The Education of a British-Protected Child: Essays* (New York: Knopf, 2009), 17.

17. Mackenzie Bell, *Christina Rossetti: A Biographical and Critical Study* (London: Thomas Burleigh, 1898), 164–65; Lynn McDonald, ed., *Florence Nightingale: An Introduction to Her Life and Family*, The Collected Works of Florence Nightingale 1 (Waterloo, ON: Wilfrid Laurier University Press, 2001), 703. The number of biblical references in Nightingale's writings is astounding.

18. Donald Harman Akenson, *Surpassing Wonder: The Invention of the Bible and the Talmuds* (New York: Harcourt Brace, 1998), 15.

19. Robert Stone, "The Reason for Stories: Toward a Moral Fiction," *Harper's Magazine*, June 1988, 72.

20. Daniell, *The Bible in English*, 516.

21. Elizabeth A. Reed, *Daniel Webster: A Character Sketch* (Milwaukee: H. G. Campbell, 1903), 92.

22. Rosenau, *Hebraisms in the Authorized Version of the Bible*, 47.

23. Christopher Hill, "The Bible in Seventeenth-Century English Politics," lecture, University of Michigan, October 4, 1991 (accessed online).

24. "William Holmes McGuffey and His Readers," *Museum Gazette*, National Park Service (accessed online).

25. Dolores P. Sullivan, *William Holmes McGuffey: Schoolmaster to the Nation* (Rutherford: Farleigh Dickinson University Press, 1994), 133. Over 130 million *Readers* had been published as of a decade ago, and the series, which has never been out of print after its first appearance, is

enjoying a renewal of interest in our day (217,000 copies sold in 1983) (ibid., 115, 214).

26. Lindbeck, "The Church's Mission to a Postmodern Culture," 45.

27. Charles Spurgeon, *The Sword and the Trowel*, 1884, quoted in "KJV or NIV," *Millennia Fever* (accessed at http://www.phenomi.net/mill-fever/index.php?kjvorniv).

28. *The Autobiography of Charles H. Spurgeon*, vol. 4, *1878–1892*. compiled by Susannah Spurgeon and W. J. Harrald (Cincinnati: Curts & Jennings, 1900), 269.

29. Alexander A. Hodge, *The Life of Charles Hodge* (New York: Arno, 1969), 404–6.

Chapter 7: The Influence of the King James Bible on Culture

1. Alvin V. Sellers, ed., *Classics of the Bar* (Baxley, GA: Classic, 1914).

2. Scott M. Langston, "North America," in *The Blackwell Companion to the Bible and Culture*, ed. John F. A. Sawyer (Oxford: Blackwell, 2006), 210–11.

3. Sanja Zgonjanin, "Quoting the Bible: The Use of Religious References in Judicial Decision-Making," *New York City Law Review* 9, no. 31 (2005) (accessed online). In addition to lists of specific examples, the author used Matt. 6:24/Luke 16:13 ("no man can serve two masters") as a test case of widespread usage.

4. Peter Lillback, *George Washington's Sacred Fire* (Bryn Mawr, PA: Providence Forum, 2006), 740–60.

5. Allen Guelzo, *Abraham Lincoln: Redeemer President* (Grand Rapids: Eerdmans, 1999), 151.

6. A. E. Elmore, *Lincoln's Gettysburg Address: Echoes of the Bible and Book of Common Prayer* (Carbondale: Southern Illinois University Press, 2009).

7. Ibid., 74.

8. Winston Churchill, *Blood, Sweat, and Tears* (New York: G. P. Putnam's Sons, 1941), 66.

9. Ibid., 216.

10. Ibid., 455.

11. *The Washington Post*, July 19, 2007 (accessed online).

12. Zell Miller, "'Deficit of Decency' in America," speech delivered to the US Senate, February 12, 2004.

13. Howard W. Smither, *A History of the Oratorio*, vol. 4 (Chapel Hill: University of North Carolina, 2000), 168.

14. Holman Hunt, *Pre-Raphaelitism and the Pre-Raphaelite Brotherhood*, vol. 2 (London: Macmillan, 1905), 351.

15. Ibid., 319.

16. Ibid., 347.

17. *The Correspondence of Thomas Cole and Daniel Wadsworth*, ed. J. Bard McNulty (Hartford: Connecticut Historical Society, 1983), 55.

18. *Blake's Job: William Blake's Illustrations of the Book of Job*, ed. S. Foster Damon (Providence, RI: Brown University Press, 1966); on pp. 55–66 Damon pairs each Blake inscription with the corresponding text from the KJV, and the two are almost completely identical.

Chapter 8: What Makes an English Bible Literary?

1. *Christianity Today*, December 1, 1978, 6.

2. This is the verdict of David Norton, *A History of the Bible as Literature*, 2 vols. (Cambridge: Cambridge University Press, 1993), 1:291–93.

3. John Richard Green, *A Short History of the English People*, rev. ed. (London: Macmillan, 1888), 461.

4. Donald Brake, *A Visual History of the English Bible* (Grand Rapids: Baker, 2008), 224.

5. Cleland Boyd McAfee, *The Greatest English Classic* (New York: Harper and Brothers, 1912), 93–94.

6. Ibid., 89.

7. Alister McGrath, *In the Beginning: The Story of the King James Bible and How It Changed a Nation, a Language, and a Culture* (New York: Anchor, 2001), 254–55.

8. Norton, *A History of the Bible as Literature*, 1:196.

9. Ibid., 1:202.

10. Quoted in ibid., 1:242.

11. Gustavus S. Paine, *The Men Behind the King James Version* (1959; repr., Grand Rapids: Baker, 1977), 169.

12. Brake, *A Visual History of the English Bible*, 204, 222.

13. Donald Coggan, *The English Bible* (London: Longmans, Green, 1963), 22–23.

14. Craig R. Thompson, *The Bible in English, 1525–1611* (Ithaca, NY: Cornell University Press, 1958), 27.

15. John Livingston Lowes, "The Noblest Monument of English Prose," in *Essays in Appreciation* (Boston: Houghton Mifflin, 1936), 11–12.

16. Margaret Crook, *The Bible and Its Literary Associations* (New York: Abingdon, 1937), 271.

17. Wilbur Owen Sypherd, *The Literature of the English Bible* (New York: Oxford University Press, 1938), 43.

18. Norton, *A History of the Bible as Literature*, 1:199.

19. McAfee, *The Greatest English Classic*, 102.

20. Reynolds Price, *Three Gospels* (New York: Scribner, 1996), 23.

Chapter 9: Prose Style in the King James Bible

1. Albert S. Cook, "The 'Authorized Version' and Its Influence," in *The Cambridge History of English Literature*, 15 vols. (Cambridge: Cambridge University Press, 1933), 22–23.

2. Cleland Boyd McAfee, *The Greatest English Classic* (New York: Harper and Brothers, 1912), 104.

3. Ibid., 106.

4. John Livingston Lowes, "The Noblest Monument of English Prose," in *Essays in Appreciation* (Boston: Houghton Mifflin, 1936), 4–5.

5. Gerald Hammond, *The Making of the English Bible* (New York: Philosophical Library, 1982), 52.

6. Charles C. Butterworth, *The Literary Lineage of the King James Bible, 1340–1611* (Philadelphia: University of Pennsylvania Press, 1941), 222.

7. Olga S. Opfell, *The King James Bible Translators* (Jefferson, NC: McFarland, 1982), 132.

8. Adam Nicolson, *God's Secretaries: The Making of the King James Bible* (New York: HarperCollins, 2003), 209.

9. Ibid.

Chapter 10: Poetic Effects in the King James Bible

1. Albert S. Cook, "The 'Authorized Version' and Its Influence," in *The Cambridge History of English Literature*, 15 vols. (Cambridge: Cambridge University Press, 1933), 29.

2. Charles C. Butterworth, *The Literary Lineage of the King James Bible, 1340–1611* (Philadelphia: University of Pennsylvania Press, 1941), 239.

3. Gustavus S. Paine, *The Men Behind the King James Version* (1959; repr., Grand Rapids: Baker, 1977), 124–25.

4. The three quotations in this paragraph come from, seriatim, John Livingston Lowes, "The Noblest Monument of English Prose," in *Essays in Appreciation* (Boston: Houghton Mifflin, 1936), 15–16; Wilbur Owen Sypherd, *The Literature of the English Bible* (New York: Oxford University Press, 1938), 41; Charles Allen Dinsmore, *The English Bible as Literature* (Boston: Houghton Mifflin, 1931), 105.

5. An excellent collection of reviews can be found in Donald G. Kehl, ed., *Literary Style of the Old Bible and the New* (Indianapolis: Bobbs-Merrill, 1970).

6. Dwight Macdonald, "The Bible in Modern Undress," in ibid., 40.

7. Dorothy Thompson, "The Old Bible and the New," in *Literary Style of the Old Bible and the New*, ed. Kehl, 46.

8. F. L. Lucas, "The Greek 'Word' Was Different," in *Literary Style of the Old Bible and the New*, ed. Kehl, 52.

9. Butterworth, *The Literary Lineage of the King James Bible, 1340–1611*, 1.

10. Henry Seidel Canby, "A Sermon on Style," in *Literary Style of the Old Bible and the New*, ed. Kehl, 24–26.

11. Macdonald, "The Bible in Modern Undress," 38.

12. Stanley Edgar Hyman, "Understanded of the People," in *Literary Style of the Old Bible and the New*, ed. Kehl, 59.

13. Adam Nicolson, *God's Secretaries: The Making of the King James Bible* (New York: HarperCollins, 2003), 189.

14. Donald Coggan, *The English Bible* (London: Longmans, Green, 1963), 23.

15. Lowes, "The Noblest Monument of English Prose," 15.

16. Thompson, "The Old Bible and the New," 45.

17. Clyde S. Kilby, "Christian Imagination," in *The Christian Imagination*, ed. Leland Ryken (Grand Rapids: Baker, 1981), 42.

18. David Daniell, *The Bible in English: Its History and Influence* (New Haven: Yale University Press, 2003), 429.

19. Francis Thompson, *Literary Criticisms*, ed. Terence L. Connolly (Boston: Dutton, 1948), 543–44.

20. Macdonald, "The Bible in Modern Undress," 38.

Chapter 11: Acclaim for the King James Bible by the Literary Establishment

1. Quotations in this chapter that are not accompanied by footnotes have all been taken from D. G. Kehl, ed., *Literary Style of the Old Bible and the New* (Indianapolis: Bobbs-Merrill, 1970).

2. William Blake, letter to James Blake, quoted in David Norton, *A History of the Bible as Literature*, 2 vols. (Cambridge: Cambridge University Press, 1993), 2:146.

3. Samuel Taylor Coleridge, *Confessions of an Inquiring Spirit* (Stanford: Stanford University Press, 1967), 43; and *Notebooks*, quoted in Norton, *A History of the Bible as Literature*, 2:163.

4. Eudora Welty, *One Writer's Beginnings* (1983; repr., Cambridge, MA: Harvard University Press, 2003), 33–34.

5. H. L. Mencken, *Treatise on the Gods* (New York: Knopf, 1946), 286.

6. George Bernard Shaw, quoted in Gustavus S. Paine, *The Men Behind the King James Version* (1959; repr., Grand Rapids: Baker, 1977), 182.

7. Kehl, ed., *Literary Style of the Old Bible and the New*, 5, 6.

8. Mary Ellen Chase, *The Bible and the Common Reader*, rev. ed. (New York: Macmillan, 1960), 23.

9. Reynolds Price, *Three Gospels* (New York: Scribner, 1996), 23.

Chapter 12: Literature and the Bible

1. C. S. Lewis, "The Literary Impact of the Authorised Version," in *Selected Literary Essays*, ed. Walter Hooper (Cambridge: Cambridge University Press, 1969), 126–45.

2. Examples include the following "standbys": *The Enduring Legacy: Biblical Dimensions in Modern Literature*, ed. Douglas C. Brown (New York: Scribner's, 1975); *Chapters into Verse: Poetry in English Inspired by the Bible*, ed. Robert Atwan and Laurance Wieder (New York: Oxford University Press, 1993); *The Gospels in Our Image: An Anthology of Twentieth-Century Poetry Based on Biblical Texts*, ed. David Curzon (New York: Harcourt Brace, 1995); *The Bible and Literature: A Reader*, ed. David Jasper and Stephen Prickett (Oxford: Blackwell, 1999); *The Poetic Bible*, ed. Colin Duriez (Peabody, MA: Hendrickson, 2001).

3. I have taken the formula *biblical presence* from a book title: *The Biblical Presence in Shakespeare, Milton and Blake*, by Harold Fisch (Oxford: Oxford University Press, 1999).

4. Thomas Hardy, diary, quoted in Julian Moynahan, "*The Mayor of Casterbridge* and The Old Testament's First Book of Samuel: A Study of Some Literary Relationships," in *Biblical Images in Literature*, ed. Roland Bartel (Nashville: Abingdon, 1975), 85.

5. Joyce Cary, in *Writers at Work: The Paris Review Interviews*, ed. Malcolm Cowley (London: Secker and Warburg, 1958), 52.

Chapter 13: Early Literary Influence of the King James Bible

1. William Riley Parker, *Milton: A Biography*, vol. 1 (Oxford: Oxford University Press, 1968), 10.

2. Harris Francis Fletcher, *The Use of the Bible in Milton's Prose* (Urbana: University of Illinois, 1929), 22; Frank Allen Patterson, ed., *The Works of John Milton*, vol. 18 (New York: Columbia University Press, 1938), 559–61; James H. Sims, *The Bible in Milton's Epics* (Gainesville: University of Florida Press, 1962), 4–5.

3. Chana Bloch, *Spelling the Word: George Herbert and the Bible* (Berkeley: University of California Press, 1985), xiii.

4. Thomas Babington Macaulay, *History of England from the Accession of James II*, vol. 2 (Chicago: Belford, Clarke, nd), 209.

5. The definitive edition of *The Pilgrim's Progress*, published by Oxford University Press (2nd ed., 1960, ed. Roger Sharrock) is an example of a scholarly edition that lists scriptural references in the margins. An example of a "popular" edition is *The Annotated Pilgrim's Progress*, ed. Warren Wiersbe (Chicago: Moody Press, 1980); it lists many more scriptural references than the Oxford University Press, and it actually quotes the biblical

verses in the margins; naturally the KJV is the Bible from which the editor quotes.

6. John Richard Green, *Short History of the English People*, rev. ed. (London: Macmillan, 1888), 627.

7. David Norton, *A History of the Bible as Literature*, 2 vols. (Cambridge: Cambridge University Press, 1993), 1:309–10.

8. E. M. W. Tillyard, *Poetry and Its Background* (New York: Barnes and Noble, 1948), 54.

9. Gerard Reedy, "John Dryden," in *The Blackwell Companion to the Bible in English Literature*, ed. Rebecca Lemon et al. (Chicester, UK: Wiley-Blackwell, 2009), 297–98.

10. This is the conclusion stated in the definitive edition of Pope's works, the Twickenham Edition. See *Pastoral Poetry and an Essay on Criticism* (London: Methuen, 1961), 102.

11. Charles Allen Beaumont, *Swift's Use of the Bible: A Documentation and a Study in Allusions* (Athens, GA: University of Georgia Press, 1965).

12. Ibid., 53.

13. *The Prose Works of Jonathan Swift* (Oxford: Basil Blackwell, 1964), 4:15.

14. Norton, *A History of the Bible as Literature*, 2:16.

Chapter 14: The Nineteenth Century

1. David Norton, *A History of the Bible as Literature*, 2 vols. (Cambridge: Cambridge University Press, 1993), 2:176.

2. Both sources quoted in ibid., 2:147.

3. Ibid., 2:146.

4. Harold Fisch, *The Biblical Presence in Shakespeare, Milton and Blake* (Oxford: Oxford University Press, 1999), 210.

5. David McCracken, "Wordsworth, The Bible, and the Interesting," *Religion and Literature* 31 (Autumn 1999): 21. McCracken believes that "Wordsworth's use of the Bible in his own poetry clearly goes beyond the . . . allusive to a more subtle influence of the King James Version on Wordsworth's style" (32).

6. Ibid., 33.

7. Daniel M. McVeigh, "Coleridge's Bible: Praxis and the 'I' in Scripture and Poetry," *Renascence* 49 (1997): 191.

8. Norton, *A History of the Bible as Literature*, 2:159.

9. Ibid., 2:159.

10. *Table Talk*, in *The Collected Works of Samuel Taylor Coleridge* (Princeton: Princeton University Press), 14.1.165; hereafter abbreviated *Collected Works*.

11. Coleridge, lecture 6, 1811–1812, quoted in Norton, *A History of the Bible as Literature*, 2:154.

12. Coleridge, *Table Talk*, in *Collected Works*, 14.1.75.

13. James T. Fields, *Yesterdays with Authors* (1871; repr., Boston: Houghton Mifflin, 1925), 94.

14. Aside from the KJV being the only common Bible in nineteenth-century America, the few direct biblical quotations in Hawthorne's fiction suggest the KJV, and additionally all of the literary scholarship on the subject adduces the KJV as an agreed-upon point of reference.

15. Nathalia Wright, *Melville's Use of the Bible* (Durham, NC: Duke University Press, 1949); and Ilana Pardes, *Melville's Bibles* (Berkeley: University of California Press, 2008).

16. Wright, *Melville's Use of the Bible*, 8–9.

17. Joseph Bottum, "Melville in Manhattan," *First Things*, October 1997 (accessed from online archives).

18. Pardes, *Melville's Bibles*, 13.

19. Hallam Tennyson, *Alfred Lord Tennyson: A Memoir*, vol. 1 (London: Macmillan, 1897), 308.

20. Ibid.

21. W. David Shaw, *Tennyson's Style* (Ithaca, NY: Cornell University Press, 1976), 27.

22. I have borrowed the link between 2 Tim. 4:6–8 and "Crossing the Bar" from Robert Atwan and Laurance Wieder, *Chapters into Verse* (Oxford: Oxford University Press, 2000), 424.

23. Kirstie Blair, "Alfred Tennyson," in *The Blackwell Companion to the Bible in English Literature*, ed. Rebecca Lemon et al. (Chicester, UK: Wiley-Blackwell, 2009), 503.

24. Bryan Shelley, *Shelley and Scripture* (Oxford: Oxford University Press, 1994); Travis Loper, *Byron and the Bible* (Metuchen, NJ: Scarecrow Press, 1978); John Robert Burns, "Thoreau's Use of the Bible" (PhD diss., University of Notre Dame, 1966); Harriet R. Zink, *Emerson's Use of the Bible* (Lincoln: University of Nebraska Press, 1935); Janet L. Larsen, *Dickens and the Broken Scripture* (Athens, GA: University of Georgia Press, 1985); Minnie Machen, *The Bible in Browning* (New York: Macmillan, 1903).

Chapter 15: The Modern Era

1. Douglas L. Howard, "Virginia Woolf," in *The Blackwell Companion to the Bible in English Literature*, ed. Rebecca Lemon et al. (Chicester, UK: 2009), 630–31.

2. Ibid., 630.

3. Ibid., 631.

4. Virginia Woolf, *Three Guineas* (New York: Harcourt, 1938), 121.

5. Ibid., 180.

6. Good examples are the following books on *Beowulf*, Spenser's *Faerie Queene*, and the novels of Charles Dickens, respectively: Alvin A. Lee, *Guest-Hall of Eden* (New Haven, CT: Yale University Press, 1972); Northrop Frye, *The Secular Scripture: A Study of the Structure of Romance* (Cambridge, MA: Harvard University Press, 1976); Bert G. Hornback, *"Noah's Arkitecture:" A Study of Dickens's Mythology* (Athens, OH: Ohio University Press, 1972).

7. Douglas L. Howard, "Woolf's Redemptive Cycle," *Literature and Theology* 12 (1998): 149–58. Jane de Gay makes a similar claim for *The Waves*, claiming that "biblical images ripple forwards into the novel as the six characters live out their early childhood . . . in a garden, until experience intrudes . . . and a version of the Fall occurs." *Virginia Woolf's Novels and the Literary Past* (Edinburgh: Edinburgh University Press, 2006), 172.

8. Virginia Moseley, *Joyce and the Bible* (De Kalb: University of Northern Illinois Press, 1967), vii. See also William Franke's essay "James Joyce," in *The Blackwell Companion to the Bible in English Literature*, ed. Lemon et al., 642–53.

9. The original sources of the statements by Joyce's brother and tutor are noted in Moseley, *Joyce and the Bible*, vii.

10. Weldon Thornton, *Allusions in Ulysses: An Annotated List* (Chapel Hill: University of North Carolina Press, 1968).

11. Moseley, *Joyce and the Bible*, viii.

12. Robert Scholes and Richard M. Kain, eds., *The Workshop of Daedalus* (Evanston, IL: Northwestern University Press, 1965), 264.

13. Interview of John Dos Passos, *Paris Review Interviews* 46 (Spring 1969) (accessed online).

14. George Monteiro, "Ernest Hemingway, Psalmist," *Journal of Modern Literature* 14 (1987): 83.

15. Studies are too numerous to list. A good starting point is Joseph M. Flora, "Biblical Allusion in 'The Old Man and the Sea,'" *Studies in Short Fiction* 10, no. 2 (1973), 143–47.

16. Patrick Cheney, "Hemingway and Christian Epic: The Bible in *For Whom the Bell Tolls*," *Papers on Language and Literature* 21, no. 2 (1985): 170–91.

17. Bhim S. Dahlya, *Hemingway's A Farewell to Arms: A Critical Study* (Delhi: Academic Foundation, 1992), 88.

18. Carlos Baker, *Hemingway: The Writer as Artist* (Princeton, NJ: Princeton University Press, 1952), 249. Baker speaks of "a slightly stylized vocabulary and movement long familiar to readers of the King James" (322).

19. Essays that explore the biblical parallels in this novel are too numerous to list. A good starting point is this one: H. Kelly Crockett, "The Bible and *The Grapes of Wrath*," *College English* 19 (1962): 193–99; J. Paul Hunter, "Steinbeck's Wine of Affirmation in *The Grapes of Wrath*," in *Twentieth Century Interpretations of The Grapes of Wrath*, ed. Robert Con Davis (Englewood Cliffs, NJ: Prentice-Hall, 1982), 36–47; and J. C. R. Perkin, "Exodus Imagery in *The Grapes of Wrath*," in *Literature and the Bible*, ed. David Bevan (Amsterdam: Rodopi, 1993), 79–93.

20. Meg Twycross, "The Theatre," in *The Blackwell Companion to the Bible and Culture*, ed. John F. A. Sawyer (Oxford: Blackwell, 2006), 357.

21. *The Gospels in Our Image: An Anthology of Twentieth-Century Poetry Based on Biblical Texts*, ed. David Curzon (New York: Harcourt Brace, 1995).

22. Scott Donaldson, *Edwin Arlington Robinson: A Poet's Life* (New York: Columbia University Press, 2007), 349.

23. Ibid., 395.

24. Marie Borroff, "Robert Frost's New Testament: Language and the Poem," *Modern Philology* 69 (1971): 45. Borroff speaks of Frost's "simple and common diction, . . . biblical allusiveness, simple syntax," and attributes this style to the Authorized Version; she also links Frost in this regard to George Herbert and John Bunyan. Dorothy Judd Hall believes that "the reverential tone throughout Frost's poetry is solidly grounded in his reading of the Bible." "An Old Testament Christian," in *Frost: Centennial Essays III*, ed. Jac Tharpe (Jackson: University Press of Mississippi, 1978), 335.

25. Victor E. Reichert, "The Faith of Robert Frost," in *Frost: Centennial Essays* (Jackson: University Press of Mississippi, nd), 421.

26. James Weldon Johnson, *God's Trombones: Seven Negro Sermons in Verse* (1927; repr., New York: Penguin, 1976), 9.

27. Jessie McGuire Coffee, *Faulkner's Un-Christlike Christians: Biblical Allusions in the Novels* (Ann Arbor: UMI Research Press, 1983), 55. Irving Malin, in a book chapter entitled "Faulkner and the Bible," cites Faulkner's frequent claim that the Old Testament was one of his favorite books. *William Faulkner: An Interpretation* (Stanford: Stanford University Press, 1957), 65.

28. Dwight H. Purdy, *Joseph Conrad's Bible* (Norman, OK: University of Oklahoma Press, 1984).

29. Ibid., 145, 150.

30. Shirley A. Stave, ed., *Toni Morrison and the Bible: Contested Intertextualities* (New York: Peter Lang, 2006).

31. Danille Taylor-Guthrie, ed., *Conversations with Toni Morrison* (Jackson: University Press of Mississippi, 1994), 97.

32. For the record, Robinson also quotes from other English translations.

Afterword

1. Andrew Motion, "Students Do Not Know the Bible" (BBC Internet news site, February 17, 2009).

PERMISSIONS

Scriptures marked as CEV are taken from the Contemporary English Version Copyright © 1995 by American Bible Society. Used by permission.

Scripture quotations marked ESV are from the ESV® Bible (*The Holy Bible, English Standard Version*®), copyright © 2001 by Crossway. Used by permission. All rights reserved.

Scripture quotations marked GNB are from the *Good News Bible* © 1994 published by the Bible Societies/HarperCollins Publishers Ltd., *UK Good News Bible* © by American Bible Society 1966, 1971, 1976, 1992. Used with permission.

Scripture quotations marked HCSB are from *The Holman Christian Standard Bible.*® Copyright © 1999, 2000, 2002, 2003 by Holman Bible Publishers. Used by permission.

Scripture quotations marked MESSAGE are from *The Message*. Copyright © by Eugene H. Peterson 1993, 1994, 1995, 1996, 2000, 2001, 2002. Used by permission of NavPress Publishing Group.

Scripture quotations marked NASB are from *The New American Standard Bible.*® Copyright © The Lockman Foundation 1960, 1962, 1963, 1968, 1971, 1972, 1973, 1975, 1977, 1995. Used by permission.

Scripture quotations marked NCV are from *The Holy Bible, New Century Version*, copyright © 1987, 1988, 1991 by Word Publishing, Dallas, Texas 75039. Used by permission.

Scripture quotations marked NIV from the HOLY BIBLE, NEW INTERNATIONAL VERSION®. Copyright © 1973, 1978, 1984 Biblica. Used by permission of Zondervan. All rights reserved. The "NIV" and "New International Version" trademarks are registered in the United States Patent and Trademark Office by Biblica. Use of either trademark requires the permission of Biblica.

Scripture references marked NKJV are from *The New King James Version*. Copyright © 1982, Thomas Nelson, Inc. Used by permission.

GENERAL INDEX

accuracy
  of dynamic equivalence translations, 64–66
  of King James Bible, 62–66
Achebe, Chinua, 89
affective power, of King James Bible, 14–53
African Americans, use of King James Bible, 107
Aiken, Conrad, 166
Aitken, Robert, 54
Aldrin, Buzz, 106
American Bible Society, 54, 87, 96
American Standard Version, 73
ancient manuscripts, 13
and (conjunction), in King James Bible, 137
Anglicanism, 184
Anglo-Saxon vocabulary, 132–33
aphorism, 155–57
apostrophe, 150
Aramaic Targums, 51
archaism, of King James Bible, 14, 62–63, 148, 150, 230–31, 232
architecture, 125

Aristophanes, 155
Atwan, Robert, 162
Auden, W. H., 161, 222
auditory imagination, 147
Authorized Version, 51. *See also* King James Bible
"AVolatry," 196

Bairstow, Edward, 110
Baker, Carlos, 247n18
Bancroft, Richard, 45–46, 47
Bartel, Roland, 176
Bartlett's Familiar Quotations, 86
Barzun, Jacques, 164
Bates, Ernest Sutherland, 165
beauty, 124, 154
Becket, Thomas á, 220
Bevan, David, 211
Bible
  allusions in literature, 170–78
  authority of, 230
  as literature, 15, 118–21, 164–65
Bible Society of India, 88
biblical illiteracy, 230

SCRIPTURE INDEX